If God Is Love

If God Is Love

REDISCOVERING GRACE IN AN UNGRACIOUS WORLD

PHILIP GULLEY AND

JAMES MULHOLLAND

HarperSanFrancisco
A Division of HarperCollins*Publishers*

HarperCollins books may be purchased for educational, business, or sales promotional use. For information please write: Special Markets Department, HarperCollins Publishers, Inc., 10 East 53rd Street, New York, NY 10022.

HarperCollins Web site: http://www.harpercollins.com

HarperCollins®, ⛪®, and HarperSanFrancisco™ are trademarks of HarperCollins Publishers, Inc.

FIRST EDITION

Please note that all biblical references, unless otherwise noted, are from the New Revised Standard Version (NRSV).

Library of Congress Cataloging-in-Publication Data
Gulley, Philip.
    If God is love : living graciously in an ungracious world / Philip Gulley
and James Mulholland. — 1st ed.
    p. cm.
Includes bibliographical references.
ISBN 0–06–057841–6
    1. Universalism. 2. Christian life—Quaker authors. I. Mulholland, James,
1960– II. Title.
BX9941.3.G85 2004
248.4'896—dc22 2004052311

04 05 06 07 08 RRD(H) 10 9 8 7 6 5 4 3 2 1

To Joan and my sons, Spencer and Sam,
and to the kind people at Fairfield Friends Meeting,
who make grace real to me.
Philip Gulley

To my wife, Angie.
To my children, Nicole, Victoria,
Teena, Zachary, and Tracy.
To my friends at Irvington Meeting.
Through the trials and triumphs of grace,
you've taught me to love more fully.
James Mulholland

Contents

Acknowledgments

Finishing a book is like sending a child to college. It is a moment full of sadness and elation, the anxiety of entrusting your book into the hands of editors, critics, and readers and the excitement of watching your book make its own way in the world. Most important, there is always the awareness that no book is completely your own.

We are grateful for the many people who encouraged, questioned, advised, and challenged us—who helped raise this book. Our wives, Joan and Angie, gently reminded us of our need to apply what we write and write only what we were seeking to apply. The members of our two meetings, Fairfield and Irvington, allowed us to test our heretical ideas on them. Many of the thoughts in this book began in sermons. Many friends read portions of this book and offered their insights. John and Becky Shonle, Shirley

Lukens, Thom Horn, and Jeff Anderson all took time to carefully critique these pages. Mickey Maudlin, our editor, offered his encouragement, helping us write graciously.

Finally, we thank all those people who've written letters, attended our speeches and book signings, and assured us that what we believe matters, that it has changed their lives for the better. We've always suspected we were not alone, but grace loves company.

A Note from the Authors

Five years ago, we began writing a book explaining how two Quaker pastors, one raised Catholic and the other Protestant, came to believe in universal salvation. That book, *If Grace Is True,* changed our lives in ways we couldn't have imagined. Readers across the country embraced the book's message and began sharing it with others, discussing it in book clubs and Bible studies, and even preaching from it (and against it). Many people thanked us for expressing what they'd believed but feared to admit—that God loved and would save all people. Assuming, falsely, that we were experts on grace, they asked us how to live graciously. This book, *If God Is Love,* is not a "how-to" manual. It is our attempt to answer one question: What could our world look like if we took seriously God's love for all people?

The greatest challenge we faced in answering this question was resisting the urge to prod our readers toward our own conclusions and affiliations. Serious damage is done when religiously inclined folk like us foist yet another *ism* on others or define too narrowly what pleases or displeases God. So, instead, we've offered a broad sketch of the gracious life and trust that you, the reader, can paint in the details yourself. It's your life, after all, not ours. Whatever is helpful, we offer humbly. For whatever is not, we ask your forgiveness.

Like our previous book, this book is written in the first person, reflecting our belief that life in the Spirit is never a solo journey, but a shared story. (Plus we simply don't like all the other devices coauthored books are forced into—like saying "we" or "Phil thinks this" and "Jim did that.") Some stories belong to one of us, some to the other, and some are an amalgamation. The principles and commitments of this book belong to both of us, often emerging out of long discussion and even a few rigorous debates.

Philip Gulley and James Mulholland

If God Is Love

1

Why Beliefs Matter

When I was younger, I thought beliefs were a private matter. I had the right to believe what I believed, and others could believe what they wanted. As long as people didn't force their beliefs on me, I was happy to allow them to think things I considered ridiculous. Beliefs weren't dangerous. It was attitudes and actions that caused harm.

In the summer of 1986, I discovered this was a naive belief. That June I was hired to pastor a small rural congregation. I'd been studying theology in college and was eager to put my newfound knowledge to work. That church allowed me to preach, visit the sick, and learn why the world won't be saved by a committee. They also taught me why beliefs matter.

My first couple of months with them went well. It was the proverbial honeymoon—we each proclaimed our fondness for the other loudly and often. There was, on both our parts, some give and take. They preferred their hymns aged like a fine wine, and so I didn't suggest they clap their hands, buy a drum set, or sing lyrics projected on a screen. They discovered I was soft-spoken and bought a new microphone rather than insist I shout. We thought any other differences were minor and easily resolved. In the third month, we found we were wrong.

I can't remember my exact words, but something I mentioned in a sermon caused an elderly woman in the church to wonder whether I believed in Satan and hell. She approached me after worship and began questioning me. Lacking a well-honed ministerial radar and eager to prove my theological sophistication, I answered her questions directly and honestly. This was before I learned that answering theological questions directly and honestly is generally a bad idea, and that ministers go to seminary precisely so we can master the theological language necessary to bewilder people when pressed to provide answers they might not like.

I told her I didn't believe in Satan. Nor did I believe in a place where people were endlessly tormented. I then told her she was perfectly free to believe those ideas. I patted her hand and turned to speak to someone else, never realizing she and I differed on far more than Satan and hell. I believed then, and I believe now, that faith is a matter of inward conviction, not outward compulsion. She believed strict conformity was a requirement of faith. If I'd known this, I might have noticed the whispers during the pitch-in dinner after worship. Instead, my wife and I left church that day grateful God had called us to such a warm fellowship, unaware I'd soon feel its heat.

That week I immersed myself in my studies and sermon preparation and the next Sunday morning arrived at church brimming with excitement. It was Palm Sunday. I planned to speak on how quickly the crowd went from cheering Jesus to jeering him. It turned out to be a timely sermon.

The head elder approached me as I entered the church. "We're not holding church this morning," he said. "We'd like to meet with you instead."

A minister with a sermon in his pocket being an unstoppable force of nature, I told him we should worship before meeting to talk. This also gave me time to figure out what I'd done. I quickly eliminated all the usual pastoral indiscretions. I hadn't had an affair with the church secretary. We didn't have one. I hadn't visited the local tavern. I couldn't afford to drink on what they were paying me. I hadn't used church stamps for personal correspondence. I had no idea why they wanted to speak with me, but suspected anything that would cause them to cancel worship on Palm Sunday must be serious.

The head elder reluctantly agreed to postpone our meeting until after worship. When the last hymn was sung and the closing prayer offered, I filed downstairs with him and sat at a folding table in the church basement. The elders were grim-faced.

"This is an awkward matter," the head elder said, "but I'm afraid we're going to have to let you go."

I asked if I had done something wrong.

"There have been concerns raised that you don't believe in Satan and hell," he said.

"That's right," I said. Then, eager to display my theological prowess, I asked if they wanted to know why.

They declined my offer to enlighten them.

I began to panic. The job didn't pay much, but I was concerned that being fired after only three months might not look good on my résumé. "I do believe in the love of God. Isn't that enough?"

It wasn't.

I realize now what I didn't understand then—beliefs matter. Beliefs are not harmless. They have the power to shape our world, for good or ill. Some beliefs unite us in a great and common good, while others divide us, reinforcing prejudices and diminishing our humanity. Religious beliefs are especially potent, shaping how we think of and act toward God, others, and ourselves.

I'd thought the idea of Satan and hell negotiable. They didn't. They considered a belief in a demonic personality and eternal damnation essential. They thought those who didn't believe in hell were deceived by Satan and destined for the lake of fire. Fearing I'd lead them astray, they fired me, giving me fresh insight into the origins of that expression.

After the meeting, I walked out to the car where my wife was waiting.

"What happened?" she asked.

"It's good news."

"What is it?"

"We get to sleep in next Sunday."

We drove home and ate dinner, then I lay down on the couch to take a nap. The phone rang later that afternoon. It was an elder from another small rural church near our home.

"We'd like you to come be our pastor," he said. "Are you available?"

"As a matter of fact I am," I told him.

I preached at that church the next Sunday. I wasn't optimistic about my prospects, figuring my tenure would be brief once they found out what I believed. So I preached about God's love for homosexuals, thinking it would shock them and they'd look elsewhere for a pastor.

After worship, I went downstairs to meet with the elders, a maddeningly familiar process by now.

"Do you believe in Satan and hell?" an older woman asked.

You'd think I'd have learned my lesson and offered some theologically obscure response, but I was still oblivious to why this question mattered. I assumed that someone at the first church had called to warn them of my heretical views. More stubborn than intelligent, I answered honestly once again.

"No, I don't."

An elderly gentleman smacked the table with his hand. "I like a man who speaks his mind," he said. "Let's hire him."

And so they did. I was there four years before leaving to pastor a church in the city. When I left, it was with a heavy heart. And from what I could tell they were sad to see me go. What made the difference?

Grace.

The Meaning of Grace

I believe in grace.

Now by *grace,* I don't mean a wishy-washy, whatever-goes approach in which one belief is as good as another. I don't mean an attitude that ignores differences and tolerates every idea. Critics are right to label such thinking as lazy and indulgent. What I mean by grace is a commitment to the most difficult and demanding of human acts—engaging and loving those who think and behave in ways we find unacceptable.

Grace is the unfailing commitment to love all persons, regardless of their beliefs.

Only grace makes it possible for those who believe differently to respect and relate to one another. Grace allows us to disagree, to challenge the damaging beliefs of others even as we are challenged, and to do this without violating the autonomy and dignity of others. Grace empowers us to embrace deeply divergent convictions even as we embrace one another. We love one another as God loves us—graciously.

Love and grace are not synonymous. Nearly everyone believes God is loving, but there is considerable debate over the width, length, height, and depth of this love. For many, God's love is limited and conditional, offered to some and not others. They believe God's love is reserved for the elect and bestowed on the obedient. God's love becomes a reward, not a divine commitment.

Grace, in contrast, is not connected to our behavior. "He saved us, not because of righteous things we had done, but because of his mercy" (Titus 3:5, NIV). Grace is God's commitment to love us regardless.

This kind of love echoes throughout history in the words and lives of many religious leaders. It was the kind of love Jesus modeled and taught. It was a love offered to the outcast, sinners, and the unloved. It was a love for both neighbor and enemy.

Jesus said, "I give you a new commandment, that you love one another. Just as I have loved you, you also should love one another. By this everyone will know that you are my disciples, if you have love for one another" (John 13:34–35). What was new was not the command to love—the Hebrew Scriptures were full of such commands—but the command to love as Jesus did—expansively.

This grace allowed those in my second church to survive the fumblings of a young man who knew he didn't believe in Satan and hell, but knew little about being a pastor. They gave me the time and space to move beyond quick and easy responses to difficult questions and develop my convictions.

Eventually, I realized the importance of Satan and hell. They represent a popular and long-standing answer to the question of human destiny—some will be saved and others will be damned. The fact that I didn't believe this suggested I'd accepted a different answer. Ironically, I rejected Satan and hell before I was able to articulate a more optimistic response to the question of human destiny. Only over time did I discover why I thought believing in Satan and hell unhelpful, even harmful.

When that elderly woman asked me whether I believed in Satan or hell, I brushed aside her question as trivial. When that church fired me, I thought its members were petty and intolerant. It took four years of seminary, many years of pastoring, and countless experiences with God and others before I understood how important her question was. She was asking, though neither of us realized it, how I interpreted Scripture, how I understood the character of God, and what I thought of Jesus. Most important, she was asking me to define the boundaries of God's love.

I regret my flippant response. Only now do I understand why my rejection of Satan and hell was so threatening. She feared that, in removing one card, the whole house might tumble. She was right.

I've spent the past twenty years picking up the cards. Only in the past few years have I put my beliefs in some kind of order. I have given her question the attention it deserved and can finally give a thoughtful answer to why I don't believe in Satan or hell: I don't believe there are boundaries to God's love. I believe God will save every person.

Now by *save,* I mean much more than a ticket to heaven. I mean much more than being cleansed of our sins and rescued from hell's fire. I mean even more than being raised from the grave and granted eternal life. By salvation, I mean being freed of every obstacle to intimacy with God. We will know as we are known and love as we are loved.

Salvation is not about what happens after we die, but what begins whenever we realize God loves us.

Although I'd argue there is room for such a belief in the tradition of the Church, the interpretation of Scripture, and any reasonable discourse, I have to admit my belief is based primarily on my experience with God. The God I've experienced loves me in ways I cannot fully comprehend or express.

I'd like to think God loves me because of my sterling character and pleasant demeanor, but when I suggest this possibility, my wife's uncontrollable laughter quickly deflates such delusions. It seems much more likely that God loves every person as much as God loves me.

I believe God is love and that everything God does, God does because of love. When this love is poured on the wicked, the rebellious, and the resistant—adjectives that fit all of us on occasion—we call it grace. Where sin abounds, God's grace increases all the more. Unwilling to abandon us, God works in the lives of every person to redeem and restore. The restoration of all things is God's ultimate desire.

This universal salvation is not an event, but a process. It is God's primary action in the world. Jesus came to proclaim this good news, to draw people to God. He broke down the barriers he encountered and refused to limit God's favor to a chosen few. The cross was the political and religious response to such radical grace. The resurrection was God's unwillingness to allow a human government or religion to have the final word.

I believe God will accomplish the salvation of every person, in this life or the next, no matter how long we resist.

If Satan does exist, he will one day repent, be forgiven, and take his proper place in the divine order. If hell exists, it won't be the final destination for anyone. It will merely be another tool in God's work to purify and redeem. Years ago, I abandoned the concepts of Satan and hell as unsophisticated. Now I reject them for a far more important reason: they represent a way of understanding God I no longer find credible.

I suspect this answer wouldn't have satisfied that elderly woman in my first church. It wouldn't have kept me from being fired. It continues to cause me considerable trouble. I've learned that many individuals and human institutions still oppose such liberal grace. Many religious people regard such theology as heresy. Others, having given up on religion, consider such beliefs irrelevant. I think both positions are wrong. I think believing in God's universal salvation can change the world.

Believing in the universal love of God has changed my world. It has changed how I talk about God. It has transformed my self-image. It has altered my attitudes and actions. It has helped me see how much damage my old way of thinking did to me and to others.

I believe much of the pain and suffering in our world is a direct consequence of a persistent belief in dual destiny—the idea that some are destined for heaven and the rest for hell. This idea led to many childhood fears and insecurities. I grew up believing I was unworthy of God's love and obsessed with earning God's favor. Shame and guilt plagued me into my early adult years.

After I became certain of my salvation, I applied the same harsh standards to others. Hell and damnation allowed me to judge and condemn those different from me. They were wicked, and I was good. If challenged, I'd admit judgment was ultimately in God's hands, but I was more than willing to offer and act upon an early prediction. My smugness often did damage to those around me, but far more frightening are the ramifications when millions share this arrogance.

Charles Kimball, in his book *When Religion Becomes Evil,* writes, "Many religious people see religion as the problem. By *religion,* they invariably mean other people's false religion. A substantial number of Christians, for example, embrace some form of exclusivism that says, 'My understanding and experience of Jesus is the only way to God. Any other form of human religious understanding or behavior is nothing more than a vain attempt by sinful people on a fast track to hell.'"[1]

Unfortunately, Christianity is not alone in this religious conceit. Muslims declare *jihad,* or "holy war." Hindus murder Muslims in order to cleanse a temple site. Palestinian suicide bombers kill Zionist settlers. Israeli bulldozers demolish Arab homes. All these acts of religious violence are defended as faithful to a God who, though called by different names, loves the elect and hates the rest. Dual destiny divides the world into "us" and "them."

This traditional answer to the question of human destiny has failed us. Satan and hell aren't the problem. It is this violent and intolerant image of God that causes the world such grief. Those created in the image of this God can easily justify nearly any act—a thousand years of Crusades, hundreds of years of slave trade, the marching of Jews into furnaces, and the crashing of airplanes into buildings. The chosen are free to do great evil to those they consider damned.

As long as religions are competing for the keys to the kingdom of God, religion will cause as much harm as healing, division as unity, war as peace. As long as any religion insists those of other faiths are damned, then love, peace, and tolerance are illusions. Killing your enemies, not loving them, becomes the divine mandate. Religion will remain the problem until we are willing to tear down our bloody altars.

The answer, according to Kimball, is for religious people to see each other as companions on the journey rather than competitors in a race with a single prize. We need to recognize each other as children of a gracious God who, though our language and experience may differ, share a yearning to be united with the One who created us. We need to develop the humility necessary to listen to and learn from each other, for religion at its best is not competitive, but cooperative, calling forth the gifts of God in every person, for our good and the good of the world.

It's time for a change.

Religion will become the solution when we refuse to do violence, in this life or the next, to those who think differently. Religion can transform the world only when love, peace, and tolerance are given more than lip service. When we believe God loves and saves every person and accept our eternal connection to all people, everything changes. We are freed to seek new answers to life's enduring questions:

How should I live?

How should I live with God?

How should I live with my neighbor?

In answering these questions, I want to suggest a new world order. I use that term knowing some conservative Christians will be appalled. They'll claim a new world order is the goal of the Anti-Christ. I've come to believe the present world order, one formed around a cutthroat division between the saved and the damned, is anti-Christ. It is in opposition to the way of Jesus and hostile to the grace of God. I want to change that world by envisioning a world shaped by God's redemptive love for all.

In the following pages, I'll share a new vision for our personal, religious, and corporate lives. I'll examine how my belief in God's universal love has transformed my image of myself, softened my treatment of others, altered my lifestyle, changed my understanding of the role of religion in general and the mission of the Church specifically, and reshaped my worldview. I'll invite you to consider how our world would be different if we focused not on heaven or hell, but on creating a new earth.

In retrospect, I'm thankful that small rural church fired me. It forced me to examine assumptions I'd accepted uncritically, to reflect on my experiences with God and with others, and to seek an answer to those enduring questions I'd either ignored or too easily resolved. I'm also thankful for the churches and people who've nurtured me in the years since. In so doing, they taught me the tenacity of grace.

It took many years for me to finally accept that if grace is true, it is true for everyone. Believing this has brought me to the border of a new and gracious world—a promised land. Isaiah described it with these words: "In days to come . . . [God] shall judge between the nations, and shall arbitrate for many peoples; they shall beat their swords into plowshares, and their spears into pruning hooks; nation shall not lift up sword against nation, neither shall they learn war any more" (Isaiah 2:2, 4).

Two thousand years ago, Jesus added his voice to those who'd come before him and invited us to cross into this new land. Unfortunately, far too many of us have feared to enter. We've wandered in the wilderness, aware of God's grace, but unwilling to allow grace to triumph. My hope is that this generation will finally wade the Jordan.

If God is love, there is no reason to live in the wilderness any longer.

1. Charles Kimball, *When Religion Becomes Evil* (San Francisco: Harper-SanFrancisco, 2002), p. 27. A wonderful examination of the signs and symptoms of religion gone bad, this book also offers a vision of religious renewal.

2

Embracing Grace

I grew up in a loving church. The pastors were compassionate. The Sunday school teachers were patient and tender. The nursery was brightly lit, clean, and full of toys. Children were treasured. There were programs for every age group, and the volunteers were dedicated and generous. I still remember when Mr. Rice let the fifth-grade boys camp out in his backyard. You have to be a saint to teach a fifth-grade boys' Sunday school class. Either saintly or crazy. Yet in the midst of all of this affection, I was taught to fear the Lord.

I don't think this was malicious. The teachers and preachers of my childhood were good people. Mr. Rice never raised his voice or threatened violence, though the behavior of fifth-grade boys is a strong argument for wrath. In between giving us candy and confiscating our pocketknives, marbles, and baseball cards, he squeezed in stories from the

Bible. The Bible, rather than Mr. Rice, was to blame for my fear.

I especially remember the story of Uzzah. King David and his court were bringing the ark of the covenant (where God's presence dwelled) from Baale-judah to Jerusalem. Along the parade route, the oxen stumbled, the cart swayed, and the ark seemed ready to crash to the ground. A man named Uzzah reached out to steady the ark. The Bible says, "The anger of the Lord was kindled against Uzzah; and God struck him ... and he died there beside the ark" (2 Samuel 6:7).

How was I to understand God's behavior when Uzzah touched the ark? Uzzah's actions were innocent; he didn't want the ark to crash. In college, I studied this story again. One scholar argued that God doesn't need our help, that Uzzah's steadying the ark indicated he didn't trust God. Uzzah's death was a brutal object lesson. Another scholar observed that the Levites had been commanded to carry the ark on their shoulders, not in a cart. Uzzah was the unfortunate victim of a bureaucratic error. None of these explanations lessened my discomfort.

Apparently, I wasn't the only one troubled by God's capriciousness. King David was also upset. He cancelled the parade and sent the celebrants away. He didn't bring the ark to Jerusalem. Even worse, Scripture tells us David was afraid of the Lord. And rightly so. If Uzzah could be struck down so easily, who was safe from the wrath of God?

Fear is the theme of many biblical stories about God. No

one in church questioned the truth of such portrayals. Fearing God was considered a virtue. "The fear of the Lord is the beginning of wisdom" (Psalm 111:10). I've since learned the Hebrew word translated "fear" denotes awe and reverence more than fright. But, as a child, I wasn't awed by God. I was afraid.

I wish I could say Christianity eased my anxiety, but the traditional theology of the Church was equally frightening. I was a sinner deserving of death and eternal torment in hell. Nothing I said or did could change my status or appease God's wrath. My teachers and preachers left no room for debate. "All have sinned and fall short of the glory of God" (Romans 3:23). They were also clear about the consequences. "The wages of sin is death" (Romans 6:23). Even before I completely understood the difference between right and wrong, I knew I was doomed.

I was also taught that Jesus loved me. He was the good news. The wages of sin was death, "but the free gift of God is eternal life in Christ Jesus our Lord" (Romans 6:23). Jesus saved us. His willingness to take our place on the cross and pay our debt rescued us from divine retribution. Later, I'd be taught God's wrath wasn't vindictive, that God was required to uphold the dictates of justice and holiness, but when I was a child these distinctions were lost on me. I simply believed God was mad, and someone had to pay.

Every Sunday we were reminded of how Jesus paid it all, how he loved us so much he died for us. The descriptions of his crucifixion were not of a religious reformer killed by the authorities, but of a friend laying down his life for us. Nearly every lesson and sermon ended with an appeal to give our hearts to Jesus. Moved by such selfless love, I did this early and often, visiting Jesus at the altar whenever possible.

My teachers and preachers praised my spiritual sensitivity, when actually I was scared to death. They didn't realize how their mixed message of fear and love disturbed and confused a young boy who craved acceptance. I was a teenager before it dawned on me that the weekly appeal wasn't aimed at me. I'd already been saved. We sang "Just as I Am" three times because someone else needed salvation. Grace was not an expression of God's affection, but fire insurance.

Turn or Burn:
The Problem with Fear

The teachers and preachers of my childhood must have thought love, although compelling, was ineffective in reaching the most resistant. Though they always emphasized God's love, they usually finished their appeals with a threat—those who didn't accept Jesus would spend eternity in hell. Some described this punishment more graphically than others, but all offered the same warning—turn or burn.

Jesus and God were presented as partners in a mission to save the world. Jesus was the good cop, gentle and sympathetic, willing to take a bullet for us, appealing to conscience and promising us a reward for doing the right thing. God was the bad cop, standing in the background with his arms folded across his chest, glaring at us. As long as we responded to Jesus, God remained in the shadows. But, should we resist, we were reminded that we wouldn't want Jesus to leave us in the room alone with God. At which point, God would crack his knuckles and scowl.

Fortunately, although the lessons and sermons were often frightening, my teachers and preachers were generally far more gracious than their theology. Mr. Rice patiently tolerated the shenanigans of a dozen restless boys. My parents, though never openly challenging this fear-based theology, spoke of Jesus as a friend and God as a loving father. I had many examples of people transformed by a relationship with God. They encouraged me to seek this God who was seeking me. Soon my experiences with God began to challenge the theology of my childhood.

The longer I was in relationship with God, the less I feared. I experienced a God who was "merciful and gracious, slow to anger, abounding in steadfast love and faithfulness ... forgiving iniquity and transgression and sin" (Exodus 34:6–7). I began to appreciate why Jesus claimed God as a loving parent rather than a remote and hostile deity.

When I understood God as a parent, it occurred to me that my relationship with my parents had nothing to do with fear. Those who feared their parents had almost always been abused by them. An abusive God frightening some into submission and eternally torturing others became incredible.

I also discovered how seldom Jesus used fear as a motivator. One of his favorite phrases was "Don't be afraid." His appeal was one of good news, not dire consequences. He proclaimed the year of God's favor, not the coming of God's wrath. Jesus attracted people with his compassion and his stories of a gracious God, not with warnings of fire and brimstone. Most important, Jesus said his attitude and approach to people represented God's heart, and because I didn't fear Jesus, I began to trust God.

One day I stumbled across a verse my teachers and preachers had never emphasized: "There is no fear in love, but perfect love casts out fear; for fear has to do with punishment, and whoever fears has not reached perfection in love" (1 John 4:18). I wasn't completely certain what this meant, but knew I didn't want fear to be part of my relationship with God any longer.

Of course, moving from a theology of fear to one of grace takes time. I wasn't immediately consistent. (And I still struggle.) For many years, I lived in this no-man's-land between fear and grace. I believed in and taught God's unfailing commitment to love, but held on to theological formulas that called this grace into question. God was good, but he'd also demanded Jesus's blood. Jesus loved every person, but someday he'd come with sword in hand and destroy many of those people. I often felt the dissonance of these beliefs, but like a battered spouse I thought love and fear unavoidable in a relationship with God.

Though I never adopted a fire-and-brimstone style, when people resisted my pastoral ministry, the threats and warnings of the past came naturally. God was gracious to me, but there were some who seemed appropriate targets for divine wrath. Theological violence, though a last resort, remained an attractive option. Yet whenever I made use of fear, I felt spiritually soiled.

Abandoning fear as a tool of ministry became easier when I saw its ugliness at an evangelical youth rally. I'd taken the youth of my church to hear a popular evangelist. The rally was far different from the revivals of my childhood—rock music had replaced hymns, images flashed on large video screens, and young people hit beach balls from one part of the arena to the other. Everything had changed but the message.

The speaker stood and told the same frightening story of sin and death. He announced the same good news of Jesus and his love. He ended with the same threats. He said, "Tonight, if you have any doubts about your salvation, if you aren't completely certain of where you'll spend eternity, and if you think there is even the slightest chance you might be headed for hell, then you need to come to this altar." Not surprisingly, hundreds rushed to the altar in response.

I noticed a disturbing pattern. The young people in our group who went forward were from negligent and abusive families. Those who remained seated came from healthy, loving families. That night I realized how fear manipulates. I recognized how Christianity has preyed on the insecure and anxious. Later I read a report of the rally that claimed four hundred young people had "given their lives to Christ." I wondered if what really happened was that four hundred emotionally vulnerable and broken young people were taught to fear God.

When I've told this story in the past, some have said that even if the initial motivation was fear, any relationship to

God is better than none, that the end justifies the means. But what end do we seek? Is the success of our evangelism dependent upon how many people kneel at an altar? Or do we judge our effectiveness by how enduring and healthy a person's relationship with God becomes?

A friend once gave me a video of the Christian play *Heaven's Gates and Hell's Flames.* The title set off warning bells, but my friend assured me I'd enjoy it. She explained that her teenage daughter, a prodigal who'd resisted her mother's religious appeals, had gone to the altar after attending the play. She wanted me to take our youth group to a local production.

The play was appalling. It was a series of vignettes in which persons either accepted or rejected the "plan of salvation" and were then unexpectedly killed in car accidents or in construction-site disasters. They would arrive at heaven's gates, where an angel would look for their names in the Book of Life. Those who were saved were warmly welcomed, while the unsaved were dragged from the gates by cackling demons. Children were ripped from their mothers' arms and husbands separated from their sobbing wives, while the cries of the damned went unheeded.

I wasn't surprised my friend's daughter responded to the altar call after viewing the play's threats of pain, torture, and separation from her family. Unfortunately, she'd heard absolutely nothing about the love of God. Her visit to the altar didn't change her. It only reinforced her hunch that God was to be feared. She soon lapsed back into the destructive behaviors her mother had hoped to rescue her from. Using fear is not only manipulative; it is also ineffective, making people even more resistant to God's grace.

Fear cripples our ability to love and act wisely. The philosopher Bertrand Russell said, "Neither a man, nor a crowd, nor a nation can be trusted to act humanely or to think sanely under the influence of a great fear."[1] There is no fear greater than that of death and destruction. A theology based on this fear seldom inspires great acts of compassion and service. When we live in constant fear of divine rejection, we focus all our attention on securing our survival. Sadly, this self-absorption only leads us further from love.

Fear and love are incompatible. Fear indicates our distrust of the one who claims to love us. A child trembles when a parent threatens, "If you don't behave, I'll send you away." A wife is terrorized when a husband warns, "If you leave me, I'll kill you." Human beings cower when God commands, "Serve me, or I'll damn you to hell." Where fear is encouraged, love withers.

My mother came from a broken family. She became convinced her father left because of her misbehavior, that she was bad and he'd rejected her. She carried this burden into her marriage. Indeed, the night before she married my father, her grandfather, who'd raised her, pulled her aside and warned, "This man you're marrying is too good for you, but if he leaves you, we'll take you back."

My father tells the story of the first night he left my

mother home alone. He returned to find her hysterical, sobbing in their darkened living room. When he asked what was wrong, she replied, "I was afraid you'd never come back." Though he assured her he'd never leave her, it took many years for my mother to trust my father's love. Only his unconditional love had the power to heal her deepest wounds, calm her secret fears, and transform her into a mature, beautiful human being. Where love is triumphant, fear ends.

Human transformation comes when love casts out fear, assuring us we'll never be disowned, abandoned, or destroyed. Only in the rich soil of unconditional love can we truly grow. Believing in God's desire to save every person calms our fears of death and destruction. It assures us of God's acceptance. Grace gives us the freedom to live boldly.

Unfortunately, most of us don't move directly from fear to grace. Many of us, myself included, take a detour through manipulation and pride. We work out our salvation with fear and trembling, negotiating with God. God may save us, but proper behavior keeps us saved. Our task is to learn the catechism, complete the rites, affirm the doctrine, and obey the rules. In turn, God writes our name in the Book of Life, prepares our heavenly mansion, and fits us for wings.

As a young pastor, though I often spoke of God's grace, I operated as if salvation were a trophy. I, and those like me, were on the winning team. We'd run the race, crossed the finish line, and won the prize. I no longer feared God, but my relationship with God was still lacking. I had simply moved from a hell-fearing to a heaven-earning religion.

Earning Grace:
The Problem with Reward

Religion focused on escaping hell's flames is ugly, but appeals based on entering heaven's gates are equally flawed. I grew up hearing as many descriptions of the joys of heaven as I did of the miseries of hell. They were also vivid, with talk of golden streets and opulent mansions, of choirs of angels and banquet feasts, and of heavenly reunions with loved ones. If hell was the stick, heaven was the carrot.

Many of the teachers and preachers of my childhood downplayed hell and damnation. Though it remained part of the formula, to be dusted off during our periodic revivals, most of the time we were tempted by heaven's rewards rather than threatened with hell's fires. If we'd accept Christ, attend church, tithe, and be a good citizen, our eternal security and blessing were assured. Life on earth wasn't easy, but our struggles earned us stars in our crowns.

This isn't a new religious motivation. One day, two of Jesus's disciples, James and John, pulled him aside privately to make a request. They asked, "Grant us to sit, one at your right hand and one at your left, in your glory" (Mark 10:37). They assumed Jesus would soon initiate a kingdom, and they were lobbying, if not for crowns, at least for thrones. They weren't embarrassed by their less than noble motives for following Jesus. The other disciples, once they heard of James's and John's request, were more jealous than angry. No one questioned the propriety of seeking rewards. They all assumed being part of the inner circle was a cause for pride and a means of blessing.

Jesus challenged his disciples. He said, "You know that among the Gentiles those whom they recognize as their rulers lord over them, and their great ones are tyrants over them. But it is not so among you; but whoever wishes to become great among you must be your servant, and whoever wishes to be first among you must be slave of all" (Mark 10:42–44). He wanted his disciples to approach religion as an opportunity for intimate relationship and service, not as a manipulative calculation designed to assure power and prestige. Unfortunately, throughout history, many of Jesus's disciples have reduced religion to a good investment.

Constantine believed his conversion to Christ secured his victory in battle. The popes promised the Crusaders paradise in return for liberating Jerusalem. Martin Luther revolted against the practice of selling indulgences, but soon offered Lutheran princes assurances of God's blessing if they opposed the Roman church. Religion, rather than being a response to God, has often degenerated into a self-serving strategy.

In the seventeenth century, Blaise Pascal made such conniving popular with his rationale for becoming a Christian.

He argued that if heaven and hell exist and we reject God, we risk eternal punishment. If heaven and hell don't exist and we accept God, we lose nothing. Therefore, becoming a Christian was the best bet.

In the United States, religious affiliation became more than a good wager; it paid a good wage. Politicians knew their election required church membership. Businessmen attended worship as an act of civic duty. Being religious was necessary to climb the ladder of success. The rewards of faithfulness were immediate and tangible. This marriage of religion and economics led to the development of prosperity theology.

This theology not only recognized human self-interest; it sanctified it. Mansions, in this life and the next, became the reward for faithfulness. The prosperous and healthy were God's favorites, and the poor and sick were to blame for their misery. If you were poor and sick, prosperity preachers promised a hundredfold increase on any donation sent to their ministries. They offered themselves as proof of prosperity even as they begged for money. Religion became nothing more than a get-rich-quick scheme.

Though I rejected the more blatant manifestations of this reward-based theology, I was hardly immune to the enticement of heavenly prizes. I believed there was a direct correlation between my behavior and God's favor and enthusiastically set out to earn God's blessing and help others do the same.

As a young pastor, I was asked to lead a midweek children's program that had about fifteen children attending. Dissatisfied with such low participation, I developed a system, modeled after one from my own childhood, whereby children could earn points for attendance, memorizing Bible verses, inviting friends, and completing projects. They lost points for bad behavior. When they had accumulated enough points, they could turn them in for prizes. We soon had as many as a hundred children coming on Wednesday nights. Since this approach was working, I seldom questioned whether it was healthy.

By this time, I had largely rejected fear as a ministry tool, but I was more than willing to build a religious program based on reward. I began to read church-growth books that suggested what I had done at a children's level was transferable to adults. Canvas your neighborhood, discover what people want, and fashion your church to meet these expectations. Appeal to self-interest and downplay self-denial. The point system and prizes were more subtle, but the intent was the same—get large numbers of people through the door.

Since this approach works, many don't question reward-based theology. Proponents make the same kind of justifications that many used for fear-based theology—the end justifies the means. So what if people come to church initially because we offer the best day care, aerobic classes, and youth ski trips, if in the process they hear the gospel of Jesus Christ?

Having made such arguments, I know their attraction. Unfortunately, in the end, churches begin to look and act like malls, and church members are trained to be consumers of religious products.

Only slowly did it occur to me that manipulating people with rewards is as inappropriate as preying on their fears. My children's program, although never frightening the kids, offered another skewed view of relationship with God. It exposed the reward-based theology from which I was operating. Religion was about winning prizes.

When we present salvation and faithfulness in these terms, we reduce them to acts of selfishness. The Trappist monk and author Thomas Merton said, "To consider persons and events and situations only in the light of their effect on myself is to live on the doorstep of hell."[2] Unfortunately, when religion adopts, rather than challenges, this motivation, we replace a religion in which God manipulates us with fear with one in which God manipulates us with rewards. Or perhaps we create a religion designed to allow us to manipulate God and others.

Today I realize how harmful such theology is to genuine relationship. If fear-based theology justifies a God who can be abusive, reward-earning theology creates religious gold diggers—people in relationship for the wrong reasons. Believing in God's desire to save every person challenged my need to compete with others for some heavenly prize. It allowed me to approach God with gratitude rather than greed. Grace allowed me to move beyond punishment and reward.

The threat of hell and the promise of heaven remain powerful inducements in many religious formulas. Accept

Christ or burn in hell! Commit a suicide bombing and earn the pleasures of seventy-two virgins! These formulas play on our deepest fears of rejection and our natural tendencies toward selfishness. Intimidation and reward persist because they work. People come to altars and make donations. Yet their very effectiveness, regardless of which religious tradition utilizes them, relies on human weakness.

I'm often asked, "If everyone will be saved, why would people behave? Why not do whatever you want?" Such questions imply that only the threat of punishment keeps people in line. The religious are those frightened into good behavior.

Others ask, "If everyone will be saved, why attend church, serve others, and be generous? Why be a good person?" Such sentiments suggest that we consider these activities as burdensome obligations rather than joyous opportunities. The religious are those willing to endure some unpleasantness in order to earn an eternal reward. What they seek is not God, but God's blessing.

Although heaven and hell are often presented as different ends on a spectrum, they share a common assumption. For those who understand all of life as preparation for heaven or hell, a loving relationship with God is secondary, if not irrelevant. God's grace becomes the ticket to heaven rather than the means of transformation. Such cynical thinking suggests there is nothing inherently attractive in a relationship with God, that without the carrot or the stick, no one would bother with God.

Yet what ultimately attracted me to God and the Church wasn't fear or greed. It was meeting people who lived their lives selflessly, who no longer asked, "What's in it for me?" They spoke of God not as an abstraction, but as one who loved them so fully they were freed to love extravagantly.

Accepting Grace

Mary Shaw loved extravagantly. She was a tiny woman with a huge heart for children. She had a passel of children and grandchildren and treated everyone else's children as her own. She cooked supper for the nearly hundred children who came each Wednesday night. While I was busy keeping track of points and buying prizes, she was shopping for deals, baking cupcakes and cookies, asking stores for donations, and using her small pension to buy milk and meat. This alone qualified Mary as an exceptional person, but that wasn't her chief attraction.

Mary knew God. I found myself sneaking down on Wednesday afternoons an hour before the kids arrived to talk with Mary as she stirred her soup and baked her bread. I'd share my problems and frustrations, and she'd offer me words of encouragement. When she spoke of Jesus, it was as if he lived at her house, drove with her in the car, and sat in the kitchen with her. Her relationship with God was full of peace and joy. When she would wrap her arms around me, her head barely reaching my chest, she'd whisper, "God loves you so much."

Mary taught me that knowing God is the prize.

Pure religion is not about earning heaven or escaping hell. It is about discerning our proper place and role in creation—that God did not create us to be cowering supplicants or greedy schemers, striving to escape this world. Instead, we see ourselves as God sees us—as the crown of creation, children created in his image, precious in his sight, capable of loving as we have been loved, and destined to dwell with God forever. When God looks on us, God smiles. Pure religion is learning to smile back.

I was never taught to smile at God. I was instructed to approach God with eyes averted, head bowed, and hands clasped. The teachers and preachers of my childhood convinced me of my unworthiness. They neglected the first chapter of Genesis with God's affirmation of human goodness and emphasized the second chapter of Genesis with its human disobedience and divine rejection. This rendering of history colored their interpretation of everything that followed. God was seen as an adversary rather than a friend. Humanity was viewed as fallen rather than in need of nurture and growth.

As a child, I was steeped in this negativity. I was taught, over and over, that I was born in sin, stained by Adam's fall, and heir to God's wrath. I was reminded often that "there is no one who is righteous, not even one; there is no one who has understanding, there is no one who seeks God. All have turned aside, together they have become worthless" (Romans 3:10–12). The good news of God's love was presented only after we'd been browbeaten into submission. In so doing, the church made a virtue of the most damaging of sins—believing ourselves unlovable.

In time, I've come to reject that view. If Jesus expected me to love my neighbor as myself, I needed to learn to love myself. This didn't mean ignoring my many faults and frailties, but accepting that I was born, not sinful, but immature, in need of growth and nurture. Jesus came not to save worthless human beings, but to articulate a vision of a God that sees all people as deserving of love. Our problem is not original sin, but not understanding our full potential. When God created us, he called us very good.

The Psalmist asks, "When I look at your heavens, the work of your fingers, the moon and the stars that you have established; what are human beings that you are mindful of them, mortals that you care for them?" (Psalm 8:3–4). I know how my teachers and preachers would have answered that question. Before Communion, we were taught to pray, "We are not worthy so much as to gather up the crumbs under thy table."

The Psalmist had a different opinion about humans. He said, "You have made them a little lower than God, and crowned them with glory and honor" (Psalm 8:5). Jesus shared his optimism. He said, "I tell you, the one who believes in me will also do the works that I do and, in fact, will do greater works than these" (John 14:12). He saw human beings as capable of living his life and more. When we see ourselves as God sees us, our transformation begins.

Pure religion sees relationship with God not as the means to an end, but as the answer to our deepest longing— unconditional love and meaningful existence. Confident of God's care, we no longer compete for God's favor, but are liberated to live as we ought. We no longer focus on escaping this world, but in transforming it. An oft-repeated saying, attributed to the Quaker William Penn, says, "True godliness doesn't turn men out of the world, but enables them to live better in it, and excites their endeavors to mend it."

A proper self-image is vital to living better in this world. When I thought myself a target of God's wrath, I lived fearfully, worried I'd provoke God's quick temper. When I considered myself a competitor for God's favor, I lived aggressively, convinced my righteousness depended upon belittling others. Only when I began to take God's grace seriously did I begin to see myself as one of God's beloved children. I finally accepted what Philip Yancey explains so well in his book *What's So Amazing About Grace?*: "There is nothing we can do that will make God love us more. There is nothing we can do that will make God love us less."[3]

Most of us don't believe this. We accept the traditional thinking: "If people really knew me, my secret thoughts, and hidden actions, they wouldn't love me." Our lives are often a series of carefully orchestrated deceits designed to make us more attractive and pleasing to others. That God, who knows every thought and sees every act, would still love us seems incredible. Only experiencing such grace can overcome our fear of rejection. Accepting that God loves us unreservedly makes us aware that the problem isn't God's disappointment with us, but our disappointment with ourselves. We want to be different.

I was a late bloomer. When all my friends began dating girls, I watched from the sidelines, unable to attract the opposite sex. I even began attending a new church, hoping the girls there, motivated by Christian charity, might date me. Regrettably, their charity was not as expansive as I'd hoped, and I remained virtuous, to my youthful disappointment.

When I did begin to date, in my late teens, I quickly became sexually active. Although those experiences were initially exciting, I soon felt guilty, cheap, and depressed after my sexual encounters. I began to pray, asking God to remove this urge from me. I was certain he was angered by my sin, and I worried about incurring his wrath and rejection. I was also disgusted with myself and my failure to be who I wanted to be.

After each tryst, I would feel ashamed and determine to be chaste. This period of virtue would last for a while, but eventually I'd lose my resolve, repeat my behavior, and then spiral through yet another cycle of depression, guilt, repentance, and chastity.

This all ended one evening while driving home from a one-night stand. Deeply discouraged by my promiscuity and feeling utterly worthless, I begged God to forgive and transform me. In that moment, while I was waiting at an intersection for the light to change, the reality of God's love broke into my life. Not only did I know I was forgiven, but I experienced the depth of God's grace in a way I had never known—that God loved me despite my failures. I then understood what God meant when he told the apostle Paul, "My grace is sufficient for you, for my power is made perfect in weakness" (2 Corinthians 12:9, NIV).

It is the sufficiency of grace that ended my fear and trembling. My salvation had never depended on my striving and struggle. It wasn't about keeping a perfect record or earning a gold star. It wasn't even about my accepting God. Salvation came in knowing that God accepted me.

To be sure, God's acceptance didn't make my promiscuity acceptable. God's love exposed the selfishness and immaturity of my "love" life. Finding this pearl of great price, I was willing to sell everything in order to possess it. I wanted to love as I'd been loved.

My experiences with God have convinced me that what kept me from becoming the man I wanted to be was not sin, but insecurity. As long as I feared God's wrath, I never trusted his love. If I fought to earn his favor, I always feared I'd fallen short. Believing in God's resolve to save every person changed all of that. I could finally relax in God's love. Like my mother, I had to finally accept that the one who loved me would never forsake me.

Accepting God's grace, like everything else in my life, came slowly. Fortunately, God gently and persistently confronted me with his love. Time and again, assumptions I'd accepted uncritically were challenged by the events of life. Discovering reality's unwillingness to adapt to me, I began to grow and change. Yet none of that would have been possible if I hadn't discovered I was on a journey. I had to abandon the idea of salvation as an instantaneous event.

Growing in Grace

I remember the first time I rose from an altar after giving my heart to Jesus. I expected everything to be different. I thought my previous temptations would be gone, my character flaws miraculously healed, and my attitude forever altered. And that happened for a few days. Until my younger brother did something that irritated me and I responded with anger.

He was quick to taunt, "I thought you gave your heart to Jesus."

"If you don't shut up, I'll give my fist to you."

This was one of the reasons I went back to the altar repeatedly. I assumed every time I failed to live graciously that I'd lost my salvation. God's love and acceptance were conditional upon my behavior. The fact that I grew up in churches with long lists of inappropriate behavior didn't help. I kept seeking the instant transformation I thought would be evidence of an authentic relationship with God.

Fortunately, the Bible rescued me from this destructive cycle. I read one day that "Jesus grew in wisdom and stature, and in favor with God and men" (Luke 2:52, NIV). This was a startling revelation. I had assumed Jesus arrived on earth perfect and complete. I'd supposed that his disciples had to be equally whole and holy. Comparing myself to Jesus, I was continually ashamed. Now Luke said Jesus had grown.

I began to scour the Scriptures for other indications that our religious life was a journey. Peter said, "Like newborn infants, long for the pure, spiritual milk, so that by it you may grow into salvation" (1 Peter 2:2). Paul said, "Not that I have already obtained all this, or have already been made perfect, but I press on to take hold of that for which Christ Jesus took hold of me" (Philippians 3:12, NIV). Jesus said, "As for that in the good soil, these are the ones who, when they hear the word, hold it fast in a honest and good heart, and bear fruit with patient endurance" (Luke 8:15).

Discovering salvation was a process rather than an event allowed me to be patient with myself. I no longer lived in constant fear of making a mistake.

I recently had the joy of watching my niece, Madeline, take her first steps. Her mother was sitting a few feet away, holding out her hands, smiling and encouraging her to come. Madeline took one very hesitant and wobbly step before collapsing to the floor. Laughing, her mother swept Madeline into her arms, celebrating her first step.

Her response is God's response.

I remember when Penny first came to our church. She was rough, emotional, easily hurt, and deeply wounded. She often said and did things that were inappropriate. One day, one of our older women pulled Penny aside and scolded her, "If you're going to be a Christian, that kind of behavior has to stop."

Why is it that when children are beginning to walk, we celebrate their every step and accept every fall, but when men and women begin their spiritual journeys, we often point out their every failure and ignore their tentative steps? This is not the divine response. God, like that mother, celebrates every step. God knows we must crawl before we walk and fall many times before we can run. God understands that some of us begin our spiritual journeys on crippled legs.

I no longer expect to live a pristine life. I understand what Martin Luther meant when he said, "Love God and sin boldly." When I focused all of my attention on keeping the rules, all I noticed was how many rules I'd broken. Once I was secure in God's love, I was freed to live in that love. My focus shifted from myself to those I was called to love. Learning to love them despite their faults taught me to love myself as well.

I've accepted my need to grow and change. I am a child of God and make childish mistakes, but it is in my blunders that I learn. I marvel that this simple idea, the source of patience in every good parent, seems largely absent from most images of God. God's response to error is portrayed as immediate and severe. Uzzah touched the ark and was immediately struck down.

I don't believe that story any longer. I am convinced our heavenly Parent not only expects our indiscretions, but sees them as opportunities not to destroy us, but to encourage and teach us. "For the Lord does not see as mortals see; they look on the outward appearance, but the Lord looks on the heart" (1 Samuel 16:7).

Once when my children were small, they came running into the house to inform me that they'd washed our car for me. Since they had never asked for buckets, rags, or soap, I was immediately worried. When I walked outside, I discovered they'd taken the dirty water from a puddle and used their hands to wash the car. The car was covered with their muddy handprints.

I didn't punish my children. I thanked them for their hard work and asked if they'd like to get buckets, rags, and soap so we could finish the job they'd started. We had a wonderful time playing in the water. What I celebrated was the desire of my children to please me. I also taught them how to wash the car properly.

What God finds most pleasing is not our human attempts at perfection, but our genuine desire to do good. Thomas Merton expresses this sentiment in a prayer:

My Lord God, I have no idea where I am going. I do not see the road ahead of me. I cannot know for certain where it will end. Nor do I really know myself, and the fact that I think I am following your will does not mean that I am actually doing so. But I believe that the desire to please you does in fact please you. And I hope I have that desire in all that I am doing. I hope that I will never do anything apart from that desire. And I know that if I do this, you will lead me by the right road, though I may know nothing about it. Therefore will I trust you always, though I may seem lost and in the shadow of death. I will not fear, for you are ever with me, and you will never leave me to face my perils alone.[4]

The desire to please God is what pleases God. Our willingness to grow and change, to learn how to live properly brings God joy. We need not fear God's rejection. We need not compete for his attention. We can be patient with ourselves and with others as we grow in grace.

Believing in God's resolve to save every person has transformed my life. The boy who craved acceptance has found it. The teenager who feared God's wrath has experienced his love. The young adult who sought to win rewards has discovered God's grace is a gift. The inexperienced pastor who offended people with his arrogance has accepted his frailty. The man who wanted so badly to please God has found himself swept up in God's arms.

I'm not afraid any longer. The road rises before me. God stands beside me. Freed from the need to compete with others for some heavenly prize, I find myself reaching out to take the hands of those around me. We are traveling toward the same destination, so we might as well travel together.

1. Bertrand Russell, *Unpopular Essays* (New York: Routledge, 1996), p. 121. Russell, a self-avowed atheist, was also a brilliant critic of religion.
2. Thomas Merton, *No Man Is an Island* (New York: Harcourt Brace Jovanovich, 1955), p. 24. This set of essays contains a wealth of spiritual inspiration and challenge. Merton proclaims an expansive love within an orthodox framework.
3. Philip Yancey, *What's So Amazing About Grace?* (Grand Rapids, MI: Zondervan, 1997), p. 70. Yancey's book is a beautiful examination of grace, our inability to accept it, and our unwillingness to extend it.
4. Thomas Merton, *Through the Year with Thomas Merton* (New York: Doubleday, 1985), p. 4. One of the many powerful prayers written by this visionary.

3

Being Gracious

My father once said, "Most people talk more radically than they live. The challenge is to live more radically than you talk." I've thought of his counsel often in the past few years. As difficult as it was for me to believe in and accept God's universal grace, the greatest challenge has been being gracious to others. I've discovered, as Jesus did, that an all-embracing grace isn't popular in many religious circles. Religious gatekeepers become enraged when you throw open the gates. This angry response has tested my graciousness.

A year before my earlier book, *If Grace Is True,* was published, a local newspaper printed an article about how my work on that book had led my previous publisher, a conservative Christian house, to fire me. The reporter asked many questions about my theology. In the article, she wrote that I no longer believed Jesus was the only way of salvation.

Had I known when I was interviewed what lay ahead, I might have answered more carefully. That sentence, though provocative, didn't adequately communicate either what I reject or what I believe. Though I no longer believe salvation is limited to those who claim the name of Jesus, I still believe the way of life Jesus describes is the way of salvation.

Unfortunately, some read "Jesus is not the only way of salvation" and assumed I'd abandoned Christianity. That isn't the case. My faith is rooted in the ground of my Christian upbringing. I've simply come to believe there is rich soil in many religions. Quaker William Penn said, "The humble, meek, merciful, just, pious, and devout souls are everywhere of one religion; and when death has taken off the mask they will know one another, though the diverse liveries they wear here make them strangers."[1] Sadly, many Christians limit salvation to those who understand God or Jesus precisely as they do. Unwilling to celebrate the diversity of God's garden, they confuse flowers for weeds, trampling the tender shoots of divergent views.

Within weeks of the article, a fellow pastor wrote and distributed a letter within Quaker circles suggesting I had betrayed Quaker and Christian principles. He demanded that, if his suspicions proved true, I be disciplined. In order to determine my orthodoxy, he requested I meet with him and others from his congregation.

It wasn't a pleasant meeting. He and his companions grilled me for several hours over my beliefs. They asked me to affirm traditional Christian confessions—Jesus is Savior,

Jesus is Lord, and Jesus is Messiah. I told them I believed all of those assertions, but not as I once did. When I tried to explain what I now believe, they were horrified. They concluded I was a heretic.

In the months that followed, this pastor led a charge to remove my recording (the Quaker equivalent of ordination) and demand I retract my statements. When others were unwilling to discipline me, some threatened to leave our denomination. They couldn't tolerate being in the same organization as someone who believed in the ultimate salvation of every person.

Those were difficult months. It is much easier to think and write about God's grace than it is to be gracious. My name was slandered, my motives questioned, my sincerity doubted, and my standing threatened. In the midst of those days, my son asked me, "Dad, why do people hate you?"

I told him people didn't hate me; they just disagreed with me. I didn't admit to secretly asking that same question. Some were mean-spirited in their attack. One person, though he later apologized, publicly suggested I be beaten with a belt—especially disturbing words when you remember that Quakers are committed to nonviolence. I had to remind myself that grace isn't tested by our friends, but by our enemies.

Grace is useless as an abstraction. When Jesus called his disciples to love their enemies, he gave examples. He told them, "If anyone strikes you on the right cheek, turn the other also; and if anyone wants to sue you and take your coat, give your cloak as well; and if anyone forces you to go one mile, go also the second mile" (Matthew 5:39–41). These may be the most difficult, and most disobeyed, words Jesus ever spoke. One conservative friend explained, "Those words weren't meant for this age. In this age, Christians are at war with their enemies." Finding myself in the middle of the battlefield, I was tempted to live ungraciously even as I defended grace.

Throughout this ordeal, I've remembered my own journey, that there was a day when I would have found my present beliefs difficult to stomach. There was a time when talk of spiritual warfare, apostasy, and heresy rolled off my tongue in my misguided effort to guard the faith. Having been a gatekeeper, I've tried to be patient.

I haven't always been successful. Often I've been tempted to respond in kind. Several fiery letters were never mailed. Occasionally, I found myself wishing for un-Quakerly things to happen to my critics. I fought my tendency to demonize those who thought differently than me. I attempted to conform my behavior to my theology—to live as radically as I'd written.

Ironically, it was one of the more painful attacks that strengthened my resolve to stay the course. One day, during one of the many inquisitions, I encountered one of my critics after a denominational meeting. It was an awkward moment. Because it was impossible for us to ignore each other, we spoke. I asked her how she was doing.

She replied, "Not very well. I wish I could tell you that I love you, but I don't."

Her words mystified me. She, a staunch defender of an inerrant Bible, seemed perfectly willing to disregard Jesus's command to love her enemies. How could she say such a thing? Then I remembered some words of Jesus: "It is out of the abundance of the heart that the mouth speaks" (Luke 6:45). Her response was consistent with her theology and confirmed the reason I ultimately rejected the dualistic theology of my childhood in which some are saved and others damned. Such theology makes it too easy to hate.

A Theology of Hate

I don't want to imply that all people who believe in dualism—that some are destined for heaven and others for hell—are hateful. I have met many kind and gracious people who believe in hell. After all, this has been the prevailing theology of the Church, and many acts of love and mercy were inspired by a desire to save those thought destined for hell. Others, committed to service, have worried less about people's ultimate destiny and more about their present misery. Many Christians are far more gracious than their theology.

Unfortunately, it is also clear that many of the ugliest moments in history have been motivated or justified by a dualistic heaven-or-hell approach to life. Many, ignoring the biblical admonitions not to judge, devote their lives to separating the sheep from the goats. Believing in hell grants them unspoken permission to hate or reject those persons who, falling outside their religious and moral standards, are destined to burn.

Traditional theology has often ignored Jesus's admonition to love our enemies and replaced it with justifications for hating, harming, and even destroying our enemies. I won't chronicle the long history of Christians torturing and killing those whose beliefs strayed from the center. What concerns me is not so much what happened, but why it happened. How did the followers of one who considered being persecuted a blessing eventually bless the persecution of others? How was the Church able to diminish, if not dismiss, the command to love our enemies?

I suspect this double-mindedness was a result of the Church's gaining power. Prior to rising to power, the Church had no recourse other than grace. Grace was the means by which the persecuted overcame their temptation to hate. It also enabled them to resist the bitterness and despair that can destroy the oppressed. Grace, in the face of torture and injustice, undercut the legitimacy of the oppressors. It exposed the ugliness of their behavior, suggesting that only by brutalizing others could their views and ideas hold sway.

One of the factors in the rapid growth of the early Church was the willingness of Christians to graciously absorb injury and abuse rather than respond in kind. This commitment inspired the early Church's pacifism, its acceptance of others who'd been ostracized, and its willingness to die rather than betray the faith. Indeed, the word "martyr" comes from a Greek word that means "to give witness." These early Christians gave witness to their commitment to grace. But what happens when the oppressed gain power?

As Lord Acton concluded, power corrupts and absolute power corrupts absolutely. With the conversion of Constantine, the Church went from the margins of society to the center, from martyrdom to seats of honor. Where once it was illegal to be Christian, it soon became illegal not to be Christian. As the Church became drunk on this temporal power, it abandoned grace and picked up the sword. Coercion and control became the preferred tools of the Church.

Though love is infinite and free, power must be carefully hoarded and closely guarded. Just as the religious gatekeepers of Jesus's day feared his friendships with sinners, tax collectors, Roman soldiers, lepers, Samaritans, and women, the Church became suspicious of any idea, movement, or person that threatened its control. Compliance became the creed of the Church.

The early Church creeds were motivated more by political than theological concerns. As William Penn is credited with saying, "Persecution entered with creed-making." Like-mindedness became a requirement rather than a goal. Orthodoxy, not love and grace, became the central focus. The Church was defining who was within its gates and who stood outside its walls. Those who believed the proper tenets were called brother and sister. Those who didn't were heretics—"those who thought differently."

Thinking differently became justification for hatred and violence. St. Augustine went as far as to suggest "benignant asperity." This was a divine mandate to kill heretics in order to save their souls and the souls of those they might have led astray. It is no coincidence that the Spanish Inquisition followed. Thousands were compelled to believe in the love of Jesus in dungeons and torture chambers.

Most Christians today reject such violent means of "converting" others, although they continue to accept the theology that birthed such madness. They fail to see how the Church's obsession with power has twisted our theology, allowing us to treat our enemies with oppression and violence. Paying a token tribute to love, the Church remains oblivious to how the marriage of Christian language and violence has coarsened our souls.

When I was six years old, I became a member of the Christian Youth Crusaders. We'd meet in the basement of the church each Wednesday night to sing songs, memorize verses, and earn badges. I still remember one of our favorite songs: "I may never fight in the infantry, ride in the cavalry, shoot the artillery. I may never fly over the enemy, but I'm in the Lord's army." We were taught to put on the "full armor of God." We had weekly "sword" drills, where we earned points by being able to find a verse in the Bible, the Sword of the Lord, before the others. My church was training small children for battle.

Though no one commanded us to hate, we were taught its stories. God looked down on the world, hated what he saw, and destroyed most everyone with a flood. God hated the people of Sodom and Gomorrah and rained down fire. God loved the Israelites and made a way through the Red Sea, but hated the Egyptians and drowned their army. Some of those same beloved Israelites were swallowed in an earthquake after fashioning an idol. God loved Jacob, but hated Esau. These were the stories I was taught as a six-year-old.

Instead of critiquing the behavior of the Crusaders, my church claimed them as heroes. Rather than teaching us about peace and reconciliation, we were recruited for the Lord's army. Even the Bible became a weapon, a sword to wield against our enemies. No one questioned hatred as an attribute of God. I grew up with a theology that defended both the violence of God and the intolerance of God's people.

What I was taught about God was often frightening, but the stories of God's people were even more troubling. Israel hated the nations around it and destroyed them whenever possible. Leviticus and Deuteronomy listed people to be hated and killed. The most chilling were those commands dealing with differences over religion:

> If your very own brother, or your son or daughter, or the wife you love, or your closest friend secretly entices you, saying, "Let us go and worship other gods" (gods that neither you nor your fathers have known, gods of the peoples around you, whether near or far, from one end of the land to the other), do not yield to him or listen to him. Show him no pity. Do not spare him or shield him. You must certainly put him to death. Your hand must be the first in putting him to death, and then the hands of all the people. Stone him to death. (Deuteronomy 13:6–10, NIV)

For those who take Scripture literally, these are difficult words. They are not metaphor, allegory, or parable. They are a direct command to kill those who believe differently or who attempt to convert you to another religious persuasion. Though most modern hearers don't take up stones, many act as if these sentiments are acceptable. Those who believe differently are dangerous and deserving of censure, punishment, and even death.

The Psalmist boasts, "Do I not hate those who hate you, O Lord? And do I not loathe those who rise up against you? I hate them with a perfect hatred. I count them my enemies" (Psalm 139:21–22). Hatred, when directed at those we have judged wicked, becomes a sign of religious devotion rather than a grievous sin. The enemy is not to be loved, but destroyed, not prayed for, but preyed upon.

We can protest that religious hatred and violence are sins of the past, but to do so we must ignore current Christian visions of the future. How do we explain the tremendous popularity of the "Left Behind" series of books? These books, which have sold millions of copies and spawned two movies, portray a future in which evangelical Christians are saved while everyone else is destroyed. They proclaim a Jesus with sword in hand atop a charging steed, initiating a violent end.

Our violent religious past and expectations of a wrathful future impinge on Christian behavior today. David Benke, a leader in the Lutheran Church–Missouri Synod, discovered this reality shortly after the September 11 terrorist attacks. He was suspended for eighteen months from his duties and required to defend himself before a variety of denominational panels. His sin was not something as radical as believing in the salvation of all people. His crime was joining with Muslim, Roman Catholic, Jewish, Hindu, and Sikh religious leaders in a prayer service at Yankee Stadium. He was accused of praying with "heathens." He said, "This ordeal reveals what I would say is the hard side of Christianity."[2]

In fairness, similar stories abound in other religious traditions. This arrogant exclusivity plagues all the great religions. Adherents of each faith hate the "other"—Christians hate heathens; Muslims hate infidels; and Jews hate Gentiles. For many, religion is how we decide who to love and who to hate.

I remember watching a talk show a few years ago in which the host had invited several neo-Nazis and their children as his guests. During the first half of the program, the host allowed these people to spew their venom at Jews, blacks, Arabs, and foreigners. They defended many of their views with quotes from the Bible, suggesting God's people had always been called to purify the world. When the host asked them about love, they quoted scriptures about hating evildoers. They said they must hate those whom God hated. It seemed God hated everyone who wasn't like them.

After a commercial break, those in the audience had their turn. Unfortunately, the venom directed at the neo-Nazis was equally poisonous. Many women stood and tearfully berated them for raising their children to hate. Others suggested they should be imprisoned or killed. Some said they were wicked and evil. One man stood and said, "God hates you!" The neo-

Nazi spokesman smiled and replied, "So we agree that God hates. We just disagree about who he hates."

I've thought about his reply often. Though neo-Nazi views are certainly not examples of good thinking, he did recognize what most of us refuse to acknowledge—his children were not the only ones being taught to hate. The reason those audience members, and so many others, find it difficult to love is because we've been taught theologies of hate. God loves us and hates those who are different from us. Our visions of heaven and hell simply mirror the boundaries that divide our world.

I was taught we were to love one another, but the teachers and preachers of my childhood suggested "one another" meant those in our church, denomination, and religion. The world could be divided into three groups—the saved, the unsaved, and the wicked. We employed exacting language to describe a person's status with God. These identifications defined our responsibility toward other persons.

The saved were those Christians who shared our doctrinal creed. It wasn't enough to claim you were Christian. You had to be the right kind of Christian, a faithful adherent of our religious code. Those within this tight circle were our brothers and sisters, and we were obliged to love them. Those outside our church, denomination, or religion were unsaved. Their names were on our prayer lists. Our missionaries went to convert them. Their salvation was our responsibility. They weren't identified as our brothers and sisters. They were "lost."

Our attitude toward the unsaved held more pity than love. We knew the truth, and they didn't. We were righteous, and they were sinners. As for loving them, we were admonished to love the sinner, but hate the sin. Hate became part of the formula. As long as the unsaved remained receptive, we were to be patient. But when someone rejected our message, we were permitted to give hate full reign. We were free to shake the dust from our feet. Our responsibility to love and reach out ended. Those who consciously rejected our tidy formulas were more than unsaved; they were wicked.

According to traditional Christian theology, the wicked included most people in the world, especially if they believed in another God or theology. And since God hated the wicked, they were fair game. It didn't matter how faithful they were to their beliefs, how much they loved their neighbors, or how gracious they were to their enemies. Committed to another faith, they were doomed to hell.

In this worldview, which in many churches still prevails, God's love is always limited. God loves the saved, seeks the unsaved, and utterly rejects the wicked. God is not the father of all. Those of other denominations or religions are children of Satan. In the Christian Youth Crusaders, I was taught to love my brothers and sisters in Christ, to pity the unsaved, and to hate the wicked.

This is the theology that made it possible for my critic to look me in the eye and tell me she didn't love me. It punishes a man for praying with his neighbors. It allows neo-Nazis to defend their hate as divinely ordained. It permits Christians to disrespect people of different denominations and despise those of other religions. It supports the insistence that some must be damned. Unfortunately, this theology of hate and division is still the predominant religious model in our world.

Why does this toxic faith persist? It was what most of us were taught, both formally and informally, making it tremendously difficult to discard even after we've sensed its inadequacy and ugliness. We also cling to toxic faith because it permits us to hate and mistreat people who mystify or hurt us. It justifies our defense of hell and damnation. Finally, this toxic faith persists because the Church has found it an effective means for maintaining power and control.

Embracing a theology of universal love requires far more than a change of beliefs. It alters our perception of every human being in the world. People can no longer be divided into tidy categories of saved, unsaved, or wicked. Rather, they are welcomed as beloved children of God, yearning for the same happiness and fulfillment that drives us all. They can never again be seen as anything less than precious in God's sight. Instead of consigning the ignorant, cruel, or self-righteous to hell, we eagerly anticipate their transformation. Instead of hating them, then, we must learn to love them.

A Theology of Love

Mother Teresa spent forty years ministering to the poor and dying of Calcutta. Though she never directly challenged orthodox Catholic theology, her willingness to care for Hindus, Buddhists, and Muslims brought her criticism, especially since she never insisted on conversion to Christianity as a prerequisite to her service. When asked why, she responded, "We treat all as children of God. They are our brothers and sisters. We show great respect for them."[3]

There is perhaps no question more important than the inclusiveness of God's love. Does God love every person? Is everyone a child of God? Should we consider everyone a brother or sister? If we answer these questions positively, we accept the responsibility to care for all people regardless of their history, race, or religion. If we answer these questions negatively, we absolve ourselves from the obligation to love those we find unlovable. We will find it perfectly acceptable for some to spend eternity in hell. We will justify hatred and participate, overtly or subtly, in the destruction of those we consider wicked. Determining our relationship to our enemies changes how we live in the world. Should we love or hate them?

The Bible reflects this age-old debate. The Hebrew Scriptures usually reserve God's affection for Israel alone. Yet there is also the command: "The alien who resides with you shall be to you as the citizen among you; you shall love the alien as yourself" (Leviticus 19:34). Some passages argued for separation and hostility toward the non-Jew. Others challenged Israel to reach out. "It is too light a thing that you should be my servant to raise up the tribes of Jacob and to restore the survivors of Israel; I will give you as a light to the nations, that my salvation may reach to the end of the earth" (Isaiah 49:6).

This tension continued in the Christian Scriptures. Though Christianity claimed Jesus as the light to the nations, the Christian attitude toward those in darkness varied. Some passages argued for a universal concern: "The true light, which enlightens everyone, was coming into the world" (John 1:9). Others claimed a more exclusive relationship with God: "Do not be mismatched with unbelievers. For what partnership is there between righteousness and lawlessness? Or what fellowship is there between light and darkness?" (2 Corinthians 6:14). The early Church often reserved the titles "brother" and "sister" for those who'd become Christian. There was little room for Mother Teresa's claim that Hindus and Buddhists were her brothers and sisters.

Who are my brothers and sisters?

Paul wrote that there is "one God and Father of all, who is above all and through all and in all" (Ephesians 4:6). This would seem a clear declaration of universal kinship.

Unfortunately, the Gospel of John says to Jesus's enemies: "You are from your father the devil, and you choose to do your father's desires" (John 8:44). Non-Christians were perceived as children of Satan. Many today continue this distinction.

My friend Gary refuses to consider a non-Christian as a brother. When I became a universalist, he was deeply concerned. He pointed out that Jesus asked and answered the question, "Who is my brother?" Jesus said, "Whoever does the will of my Father in heaven is my brother and sister and mother" (Matthew 12:50). Gary argued that only Christians do the will of God and are therefore the only brothers and sisters.

Ironically, Gary ignored the most obvious challenge to his conclusion—Jesus's words were spoken to Jews. More important, he missed the inclusiveness of Jesus's understanding of kinship. Jesus spoke those words at the end of a long series of encounters with his opponents. They were critical of his interaction with those they considered outcast—lepers, Romans, the blind and mute, tax collectors, and other sinners. When he healed a demon-possessed man, they accused him of being a fraud in league with Satan. At the core of his debate with his peers was the question of who God loved.

When Jesus redefined kinship, he was challenging their exclusive circles by declaring that anyone in any place who did the will of God, regardless of social standing or religious affiliation, was his brother or sister. Kinship was not a matter of racial, religious, or cultural conformity. It was the by-product of a commitment to the will of God—to love and care for all.

A theology of love begins with the assumption that all people are God's cherished children and deserving of love. "We love because he first loved us. Those who say 'I love God,' and hate their brothers and sisters, are liars, for those who do not love a brother or sister whom they have seen, cannot love God whom they have not seen" (1 John 4:19–20). Jesus demonstrated his love for the outcasts, those many considered unlovable. Regrettably, many Christians have been unwilling to adopt the ethic of Jesus—a theology of inclusion, acceptance, and love. We've been unwilling to love and accept our enemies. We haven't even been excited about loving our neighbor.

One day, a lawyer stood up to test Jesus. "Teacher," he asked, "what must I do to inherit eternal life?"

Jesus said to him, "What is written in the law? What do you read there?"

He answered, "You shall love the Lord your God with all your heart, and with all your soul, and with all of your strength, and with all of your mind; and your neighbor as yourself."

And Jesus said to him, "You have given the right answer; do this, and you will live" (Luke 10:25–28).

Many Christians ignore this clear definition of salvation. Jesus didn't suggest salvation was a matter of theological orthodoxy, doctrinal purity, or religious loyalty. He didn't offer a four-step spiritual formua, speak of the One True

Church, or give an altar call. He didn't even demand the lawyer follow him. Instead, he said eternal life is realized when we love. Of course, love is a daunting challenge. It is no wonder the lawyer sought a loophole, as have many religious persons since.

The lawyer asked, "And who is my neighbor?" (Luke 10:29). Jesus went on to tell the story of a man robbed and left for dead on the side of the road. He described two religious leaders who saw the man and crossed to the other side of the road. Then he spoke of a Samaritan, a wicked outsider, who stopped to care for the man, bandaging his wounds and taking him to a place of safety and healing.

Jesus then asked, "Which of these three, do you think, was a neighbor to the man who fell into the hands of the robbers?"

The lawyer said, "The one who showed him mercy."

Jesus said to him, "Go and do likewise" (Luke 10:36–37).

In this story, Jesus makes it clear who the neighbor is—everyone, even those we consider wicked. Indeed, they may even be better neighbors than we are. We are commanded to do what the good Samaritan did—to love all people, including our neighbors, and especially our enemies.

Of course, we continue to look for loopholes. Some believe we should care for the man who was robbed, but hate and destroy the robbers. The demands of justice trump our obligation to love and narrow our neighborhood. Criminals aren't our neighbors. Tyrants should be assassinated. Child molesters should be locked up forever. Terrorists should be hunted down like animals.

This is why Jesus insisted we love our enemies. He knew how persistently we try to escape the command to love. We always seek a rationale for hatred and violence. Jesus said, "You have heard that it was said to those of ancient times, 'You shall not murder'; and 'whoever murders shall be liable to judgment.' But I say to you that if you are angry with a brother or sister, you will be liable to judgment; and if you insult a brother or sister, you will be liable to the council; and if you say, 'You fool,' you will liable to the hell of fire" (Matthew 5:21–22).

These words initially mystified me. Having grown up on the rhyme, "Sticks and stones may break my bones, but words can never hurt me," I thought Jesus's comparison of name-calling with murder far-fetched. I suppose some of my discomfort was realizing that, though I'd never murdered anyone, I'd slung my share of mud.

In college, I happened upon the writings of Clarence Jordan, a Southern Baptist preacher and Bible scholar who left his teaching position to focus his energies on helping poor African American farmers in southern Georgia. Rejecting the learned counsel of his religious peers, he decided to take Jesus's commands seriously, sell all he had, and give the money to the poor. He thought those words the core of the Christian ethic. In explaining the passage above, Jordan writes:

Jesus is saying, then, that murder really begins when one loses his respect for human personality and the infinite worth of every individual. . . . If a person convinces himself that the lives of others aren't worth much, the inference is drawn that it does not matter particularly what happens to them. They may be shot, they may be exploited, or bombed, or they may be used as cannon fodder, and it's perfectly all right.[4]

Jordan's words not only shed light on this passage; they helped me understand the importance of name-calling. Believing certain people are fools is merely the first step in justifying their eventual murder. Such thinking is always necessary to overcome our inhibition against shedding blood. Yet if Jesus is right, name-calling can be the beginning of peace and reconciliation as well as of hatred and murder.

What we call one another matters. If we call others unsaved, wicked, sinners, pagans, or heathens, we no longer recognize them as children of God. This demonizing of the enemy has been part of every genocide, massacre, war, or oppression. Too often, religion, rather than reminding nations and peoples of their common humanity, has been in the forefront of this name-calling. The assumption that those we have declared demonic are destined to hell makes justifying their destruction even easier.

But if we call them neighbors, brothers, sisters, or

friends, we begin to see their humanity and our responsibility to love and care for them. We recognize what Cain tried to ignore—we are our brother's keeper.

A theology of love is grounded in the realization that God loves our enemies as much as God loves us. And we are all created in the image of this God. We are all precious in God's sight. We are all children of God. This, more than any other idea, changes how we perceive others. It requires us to call every man and every woman by the names that make murder nearly impossible—brother and sister. This is the irony of Jesus's command to love our enemy. Once we perceive our enemies as our brothers and sisters, they cannot remain our enemies. Once we see our kinship to all, we no longer see them as competitors for God's favor, but as fellow heirs of an expansive grace.

The Power of Empathy

A young man named Francis, while riding his horse one day, encountered a leper. He and the leper shied away from each other—the leper because he expected abuse and Francis because he was repulsed by the man's disfigurement and feared the disease. But something extraordinary happened on that road. Francis reported that as he looked upon that leper something changed inside him. Suddenly, he found he loved the leper. He dismounted from his horse, embraced the leper, and gave him all the money he had. He was filled with kindness, and his life was never the same.

Soon after this episode, Francis visited Rome and found himself drawn not to the marvelous buildings, marble statues, or gem-encrusted crosses. Instead, he spent his time among the beggars who wandered the Holy City, listening to their stories and experiencing the sneers and catcalls of those entering the cathedrals to honor God. He returned from Rome and began to pray. He found his prayers answered when one day he attended Mass and heard the Gospel lesson in which the disciples of Christ are commanded to possess "neither gold, nor silver, . . . nor scrip for

[the] journey, neither two coats, neither shoes, nor yet staves" (Matthew 10:9–10, KJV). Francis knew those words were for him.

Francis of Assisi preached to birds, begged forgiveness from wolves, and shared his bowl with the poor. He was a bright light in a dark age. His Franciscan order, established in 1208, has touched the lives of millions. His rule was simple: "Whoever may come to us, whether a friend or foe, a thief or a robber, let him be kindly received. Should there be a brother anywhere in the world who has sinned, no matter how great his fault, let him *not* go away after he has once seen thy face, without showing mercy toward him."

My greatest challenge isn't believing God will save every person. It is treating each and every person as a child of God. It is remembering this wonderful grace, which has overwhelmed and transformed me, is also at work in every other person. It is seeing the worst of sinners as the beloved of God.

This is never easy. Several years ago, I struck up a friendship with a man in prison. Curt was a member of a Bible study I taught. He was intelligent, articulate, and well versed in theology. He had a quick wit and a good sense of humor. When he was released from prison, we continued our friendship.

Early in our friendship, I discovered Curt has been convicted of child molestation. Having worked with others who had committed this crime, I thought myself immune to revulsion. When Curt told of his relationship with his victim—the manipulation, the coercion, the sexual activity—I imagined all of this occurring with a teenage boy. When Curt told me his victim had been five, I couldn't hide my shock and dismay. In that moment, I realized the challenge of loving every person. It took everything in me not to call Curt a pervert.

Of course, calling him this would have ended our friendship, declared him less than human, and absolved me from treating him as a child of God—a broken and flawed child of God, but a child of God nonetheless. My belief that he and I would spend eternity together required I not turn my back on him. Instead, I committed myself to being part of his transformation.

The abhorrent nature of his crime made his need for my love and acceptance even more crucial. We know those who molest children often repeat their crime. Without friends who love and challenge them, they are far more likely to hurt another child. I suspect one of the reasons so many sexual offenders repeat their crimes is because we ostracize them rather than help them heal.

This is why Jesus's treatment of the lepers is so important to Christian ethics. Leprosy was not understood in that time as a physical ailment. It was seen as a punishment from God for some heinous sin. The willingness of Jesus to forgive, touch, and heal lepers is more than an argument for his supernatural abilities. It is a proclamation of his theology. God loves all people. Even those we find abhorrent.

Of course, being gracious to others comes not just when

we believe God loves them as much as God loves us. It also requires us to remember that within each of us, given different circumstances, resides the potential for both great evil and great good.

Whenever I tell the story of Curt, I realize some won't accept or understand my love for him. Some have been victims of sexual molestation themselves and, having yet to experience healing, will find it difficult to feel any emotion other than loathing for him. Others will reject him because they fear the damage he might do to them or those they love. Still others, never having experienced his struggle, will judge him depraved. Pain, fear, and pride are enemies of grace. They make it impossible for us to forgive, to risk relationship, and to consider our own frailty. The only way to overcome these obstacles is empathy.

Curt's story didn't begin with his molestation of a five-year-old. It began with a lonely childhood, an emotionally distant father, a series of sexual experiences that distorted Curt's understanding of appropriate behavior, a troubled marriage, and a set of circumstances that allowed Curt to spend many unsupervised hours with this young boy. None of these facts excuses Curt's behavior, but all of these contributed to his crime.

The only reason I was able to remain in relationship with Curt was because I was able to empathize with him. Instead of seeing him as a forty-year-old man taking sexual advantage of a child, I chose to see him as a lonely boy, a neglected child, an abused teenager, and a troubled and broken adult.

Being gracious to Curt required me to see him as a person struggling to love and be loved and not knowing how.

This empathy didn't trivialize Curt's crime. It simply reminded me of our common humanity. It created the space for love and transformation. Being gracious is more than accepting outcasts. It is seeking ways to heal them and restore them to community. My love for Curt meant listening to his story, offering my friendship, and doing all in my power to help him confront and deal with whatever had twisted his sexuality. The most effective means of transforming those we abhor is by being gracious to them.

Empathy walks hand and hand with grace. As long as I guarded the gates of my life carefully, allowing only those who were like me into my relationships, my home, and my heart, I could find reasons to be ungracious. As long as I allowed hate, pain, fear, or pride to keep others at a distance, they remained strangers—different, and therefore a threat. Only by befriending neighbors, strangers, and enemies do we begin to understand and love them.

I am often asked how God can love every person. God loves every person because God knows every person. C. S. Lewis writes:

> If you are a poor creature—poisoned by a wretched upbringing in some house full of vulgar jealousies and senseless quarrels—saddled, by no choice of your own, with some loathsome sexual perversion—nagged day in and day out by an inferiority

complex that makes you snap at your best friends—do not despair. He [God] knows all about it. You are one of the poor whom He blessed. He knows what a wretched machine you are trying to drive. Keep on. Do what you can. One day (perhaps in another world, but perhaps sooner than that) he will fling it on the scrap heap and give you a new one. And then you may astonish us all—not least yourself: for you have learned your driving in a hard school.[5]

Many of us find it easy to judge and hate because we've not made the effort to know and understand. We assign people to hell who've spent their lives trying to climb out. Our judgments aren't based on knowledge, but on ignorance and prejudice. Yet, in my experience, the more I know of individuals, the less I feel able to judge them and the more I am able to be gracious. Of course, sometimes we don't know what causes people to do what they do. And we never will. Still, empathy doesn't require specific knowledge, but the understanding that each of us fights our hidden demons.

Many years ago, a woman phoned my home wanting to speak with me. I had avoided her in the past because of her gruff demeanor. She seldom smiled and was usually brusque and curt when I tried to engage her in conversation. I'd assumed she didn't like me and was surprised to hear her voice when I picked up the phone.

Her husband, she informed me, had had multiple affairs over the course of their marriage. That day, she'd learned of another affair. As she spoke of her husband's betrayal and her pain, I encouraged her to divorce him. That was easy counsel for me to offer—I didn't know the man and, after listening to her, didn't think well of him.

For whatever reason, the woman declined to heed my advice, choosing to remain with her husband. Several months later, he began attending church with her. Although she appeared to have forgiven him, I still bore a grudge and would occasionally insert barbed warnings against adultery in my sermons while glancing in his direction.

Apparently, he didn't take it personally, because he kept coming to church. As he changed, so did his wife. A smile replaced her usual frown. In time, I got to know him and discovered, despite his history of unfaithfulness, he was a wonderful man who now seemed committed to his wife. Eventually, we became friends.

I've never spoken with him about his affairs. To this day, I don't know the inward compulsions that drove him to abuse the love of his wife. I probably will never know. But then, empathy isn't about knowing all the sordid details of another's life. It is about remembering our own faults and failures and realizing others have theirs. It means rejoicing with those who rejoice and mourning with those who mourn, even when what they mourn is their own inability and weakness.

Having never had an affair, I found it easy to judge a man who did. But grace requires we be as patient with others as we want others to be with us. I once sat at a stoplight after a one-night stand and grieved my inability to change my sexual behavior. Grace assumes that deep in the heart of every person is the desire to be redeemed, especially from the hidden demons that torment and degrade us.

A belief in the ultimate salvation of every person is more than simply speculation about the afterlife. It is a declaration of God's work in every life in the here and now. It is a commitment to sharing that passion and participating in God's gracious activity in the world. It is being confident of God's ability to complete the work God has begun in every person. It is realizing how our acceptance of others plays a part in their transformation. Believing in the salvation of all persons changes how we perceive God, ourselves, and those around us. It alters the way we live in both the profound and mundane. It has the potential to make us better persons, citizens, friends, children, siblings, spouses, or parents. It is a belief that matters.

1. William Penn, *Some Fruits of Solitude: Wise Sayings on the Conduct of Human Life* (Scottsdale, PA: Herald Press, 2003).
2. "9/11 Interfaith Prayer Minister Reinstated," *Charisma News Service,* May 14, 2003.
3. Mother Teresa, *My Life with the Poor* (San Francisco: HarperSanFrancisco, 1987), p. 22. Mother Teresa was one who lived far more radically than she talked.
4. Clarence Jordan, *Sermon on the Mount* (Valley Forge, PA: Judson Press, 1952), p. 55. Jordan is perhaps one of the most profound, yet relatively unknown, preachers and teachers of the twentieth century.
5. C. S. Lewis, *Mere Christianity* (New York: MacMillan, 1943), p. 181. This Christian classic, though lacking the deeper insights of Lewis's later work, still offers many wonderful images and thoughts.

4

Living Graciously

Several years ago, a friend phoned to tell me he and his wife were expecting their first child. While his wife was pregnant, my friend would wax poetic about the joys of being a parent—holding his son, watching his first steps, hearing him say "Daddy," playing catch in the side yard, going to his first Little League game, camping trips, and other anticipated delights. Not wanting to dampen his enthusiasm, I didn't mention dirty diapers, ear infections, colic, and the jarring loss of freedom and spontaneity.

Three weeks after his daughter was born, I stopped by his home to visit. He was slumped in a chair, bleary-eyed and exhausted. His daughter, confused about night and day, had kept them up four nights in a row. I asked him how things were going.

"Remind me again why I wanted to be a father," he said.

Of course, he loved his daughter deeply and soon experienced many of the joys he'd anticipated. What he hadn't expected was how radically the birth of his daughter would impact his every moment, waking or sleeping.

Every momentous event, whether welcomed or resisted, has the power to unsettle us, to alter our lives in ways we'd never choose or desire. The birth of a child is not the only such moment. Starting a new job, getting married, moving to a new place, going to college, joining a church—all of these, though welcome, have the potential to stretch us, sometimes uncomfortably so. Those transitions we don't choose are even more difficult.

Altering my theology was as unsettling as any change in my life.

I went through a period when I couldn't pray. I'd been taught since birth to begin each prayer with "Dear Jesus." Jesus was my mediator—the one I pictured and addressed. When I began to question his role, I found myself unable to pray. This was painful, and I struggled for months. One day, as I tried to solve my dilemma, I imagined Jesus's coming to me and saying, "It's all right. Do what I did. Pray to my Father." The logjam broke, and my prayer life flourished again. I hadn't anticipated how my theological questioning would impact what I'd long taken for granted—my prayer life.

This wrestling with our theology, though absolutely necessary to spiritual growth, often puts our lives out of joint. On several occasions, I thought, "Remind me again why I wanted to question and challenge the beliefs I was taught." The answer, as with all change, is because what had once satisfied no longer filled me with joy and peace. This spiritual dissatisfaction is a divine gift. God loves us too much to let us remain less than we can be. Life is designed to challenge our inadequate beliefs and behaviors. Fortunately, God also guides and directs us in new ways. I discovered different answers to questions I'd thought forever settled.

As with any significant change, I welcomed many of these theological adjustments. What I didn't anticipate was how a richer understanding of God's universal love jarred every facet of my life. I naively thought I could change my beliefs about human destiny without seriously altering my other opinions. I was wrong. Once change was set in motion, many assumptions I'd held uncritically toppled down like dominoes. Believing in the salvation of all people changed my world.

This change of thinking—what some call a paradigm shift—affected my views on religion, Christianity, politics, economics, justice, and international affairs. Those are important topics and worth considerable thought and discussion. Our beliefs about such things influence the direction of our world. I've written this book convinced that if enough people discovered and accepted God's unconditional love, our world would be transformed. I'll spend much of the remainder of this book exploring the possibilities for that transformation.

However, these universal hopes are tempered by a personal reality. Paul said, "I do not understand my own actions. For I do not do what I want, but I do the very thing I hate" (Romans 7:15). This is my struggle. The solutions I so glibly offer to the world's problems lack credibility if I'm unwilling or unable to live graciously with my family and friends, in my vocation, and even in my leisure. In the end, my first challenge is to allow God's unfailing grace to change my daily life.

Charity Begins at Home

When the phone rang, I looked up in frustration. I'd spent the day working on a sermon on love and marriage. The sermon was nearly completed, lacking only a closing illustration. Now, after an hour of staring at the computer monitor, I was still at a loss. I didn't welcome an interruption.

When I picked up the phone, my wife was on the other end. She was calling to ask if I could pick up our son from school. He was ill. I quickly informed her I was very busy working on my sermon and couldn't possibly leave. She apologized for interrupting me and said she'd get him in between making our dinner, washing our clothes, and cleaning our house. Remarkably, she said all of that without a hint of sarcasm.

I hung up the phone and tried to concentrate once more on a closing illustration for my sermon. I read the last words I'd written before the phone rang: "We are called to love our spouses as we love ourselves. We are called to serve them." With that divine nudge, I phoned my wife to tell her I would pick up our son. Charity, after all, begins at home.

"If someone does not know how to manage his own household, how can he take care of God's church?" (1 Timothy 3:5). I appreciate this sentiment, even though I wish

Paul had used the word "love" rather than "manage." As a pastor, I've discovered my primary task is to be a gracious spouse and parent. How I live with my family is an important indication of what I value and believe. How I treat my wife and children reveals my vision of God and the divine order.

Unfortunately, in the churches of my childhood, men were taught to "manage" their families. Husbands were expected to control their wives and children. Order, rather than compassion and grace, were the signs of a godly home. Well-behaved children were prized. Submissive wives were applauded as women of virtue. In many homes, including my own, male dominance was compassionate and gentle. However, within such thinking were the seeds of abuse, coercion, disrespect, and fear.

I invited a woman to church one day. She politely informed me she would never enter a church again. She didn't think churches were safe. Intrigued, I asked why.

She told me she'd attended a church for years. She'd also spent many of those years in a physically and verbally abusive marriage. In desperation, she finally went to speak to her pastor about her husband—a deacon in the church. After she'd poured her heart out, the pastor listed her husband's many contributions to the church, forbade her to divorce, and suggested she wear less makeup. She eventually left her husband, the church, and religion completely. I told her she made the right decision. When religion becomes a means of oppression and abuse, we must flee as far away as possible.

She said, "My greatest sadness is that the church encouraged my husband's behavior."

Initially, I thought such stories and men aberrations. Over time, I've discovered how traditional beliefs about God's character and human destiny warp our closest relationships. I love my parents and siblings. I love my wife and children. I love my friends. This was true when I believed some people were destined for heaven and some for hell. What I didn't recognize was how the belief that some will be saved and others damned influenced my treatment of my wife and children. When I understood the character of God incorrectly, I fashioned my own character badly. When I perceived God's relationship with me as controlling and demanding, I transferred those errors to my relationships with those I loved. When I feared my own rejection, I was even more frightened about the possible damnation of my loved ones.

When I was growing up, I was taught that men were the head of the household. Paul writes: "Wives, be subject to your husbands as you are to the Lord. For the husband is the head of the wife just as Christ is the head of the church, the body of which he is the Savior" (Ephesians 5:22–23). I know men who've never set foot in a church who can quote that scripture. Unfortunately, such scriptures, rather than reflecting God's hope for relationships, reflect the influence of a patriarchal and hierarchical society in which power and control rather than grace held sway.

This masculine theology was well ordered from heaven to earth. God was in heaven. Jesus came to earth. When he ascended into heaven, he left us the Holy Spirit. Father, Son, and Holy Ghost were all described with male pronouns. They were listed in order of importance. God sent his son, Jesus, who delegated this authority to the Holy Spirit. We petitioned God through the Holy Spirit in Jesus's name. Unfortunately, as Gloria Steinem has so eloquently noted, "If God is a man, then man is God."

We may cringe at such a charge, though how can we deny it? On earth, bishops and pastors, who were all men, were the representatives of God. God spoke to them. They spoke to the congregation. Men were the heads of their households. Women were to be submissive to the men. They were never allowed to teach or preach when men were present. Children were to be seen and not heard, especially during the Sunday morning sermon. In this system, family life allegedly imitated the divine order.

This hierarchical system might be tolerable if those in positions of power are benevolent, gracious, and respectful. However, it is a dangerous approach when those in power see God as severe, rigid, judgmental, intolerant, jealous, and condemning. If God rejects the disobedient, a bishop or pastor can excommunicate a parishioner. If God can smite the rebellious, a husband can hit his wife. If God can destroy his children, a parent can justify abusing a child, who will turn and kick the dog. Even when power isn't used harshly, relationships defined by power rather than love are fraught with peril.

I was recently flipping through the television channels

when the program of a prominent pastor caught my attention. He was telling how he'd planted his first church. He said, "In the beginning, our church met in my living room. The only people attending were those I could control—my family." I was struck by how he described his family— *those he could control.* Not those he loved or who loved him. I suspect this pastor still sees those within his church as those under his control. This approach contributes to Catholic priests abusing children and to Protestant pastors having affairs with parishioners. Sadly, this obsession with control is reflective of traditional Christianity.

In dualistic theologies, everyone is either under divine control (saved) or in rebellion (unsaved). God's intention is to restore the creation to pristine order at all costs. This order, rather than reconciliation with his children, is God's primary commitment. God seeks conformity and control rather than relationship. God orders and demands rather than encourages and supports. Resistance isn't tolerated, and patience is limited. To hell with those who get in the way. When the character and will of God are understood in these terms and when men are trained in this path, grace is often the first casualty.

When I was first married, my wife and I fought often. In retrospect, many of those fights were the result of my subconscious attempts to control her. Though I had rejected the harsher versions of male religious dominance, I still thought I should have the final word. I considered myself the spiritual leader of our home.

After one particular fight, my wife suggested our marriage was unhappy. Deeply offended, I replied, "How can you say that? There are plenty of marriages worse than ours."

My wife said, "There will always be marriages worse than ours. I was hoping for something better."

On that day, I committed myself to bettering our marriage. One of the first steps was treating my wife as a spiritual partner, capable of teaching and leading me, rather than as a spiritual subordinate. This meant abandoning any theology that sanctified my inclinations toward control and manipulation. Those desires always led me to harm those I loved. Whether as a spouse, a parent, or a pastor, I had to learn to love unselfishly.

Thomas Merton diagnosed my problem. He wrote:

"A selfish love seldom respects the rights of the beloved to be an autonomous person. Far from respecting the true being of another and granting his personality room to grow and expand in its own original way, this love seeks to keep him in subjection to ourselves. It insists that he conform himself to us, and it works in every possible way to make him do so."[1]

I began to examine all the primary relationships in my life. In what ways did I insist my wife submit to me? How did I inhibit the growth of my children with my fears, prejudices, and desire to mold them into my own image? As a pastor, did I see my parishioners as dumb sheep or as fellow travelers on a spiritual journey? Was I willing to give up my quest for control? Was I willing to give my wife, children, and friends room to grow, to be different from me?

It helped that my parents had encouraged more than ordered. Marrying a talented and independent woman challenged my selfishness. Churches that didn't expect their pastors to stand on pedestals tempered my temptation toward power. Most of all, my growing awareness of God's unconditional love for me enabled me to love others more fully. If God wasn't severe, rigid, judgmental, intolerant, jealous, and condemning, I had no excuse for such behavior. If God was patiently and graciously working in the lives of all people to draw them toward wholeness, I too must love them with such tenacity.

It's unfortunate more men haven't memorized Ephesians 5:25, in which Paul writes, "Husbands, love your wives, just as Christ loved the church and gave himself up for her." Instead of promoting power and control, this verse suggests a relationship of sacrifice, service, and humility. Jesus is an example of this authentic love, which washes the feet of its disciples, serves rather than demanding service, and considers others worthy of the deepest respect.

In Dan Brown's best-selling novel, *The Da Vinci Code,* he suggests Jesus was married to Mary Magdalene.[2] In fairness to his critics, the historical evidence for such a claim is weak. It is the theological argument that is much stronger. How credible are Jesus's words about love and marriage unless he experienced the joy and struggle of this most intimate of human relationships? I don't know whether Jesus was married or not, but it's clear he understood himself as a servant as much as a leader. When we take up the crown and scepter, we ignore the example of Jesus and do damage to those around us.

I no longer seek to control my wife. (Well, at least not as often.) I try to create the space for her to question, explore, and become the person God intends her to be—a person who, thank God, is quite different from me. I encourage and challenge, but try not to manipulate or compel. I no longer see our differences as a threat, but as a gift. They help me see the world in new ways.

This transition was more difficult with my children. In one sense, a parent does have a responsibility to "train up a child in the way he should go" (Proverbs 22:6, KJV). We must teach our children to move from self-absorption to a genuine respect for the needs of others.

All the great religions try to instill certain core values in their children—nonviolence, honesty, and compassion. Regrettably, all the great religions have limited the scope of these core values by carefully defining who merits love and who doesn't. But whenever we compromise our core values, we have moved from training to indoctrination, in which "right" thinking and conformity are valued over grace.

Often, this indoctrination is motivated by a desire to control and manipulate. Some parents seek to mold their children into copies of themselves. They see their children's individuality as a threat and demand their total submission. Religion, for these parents, is a manipulative tool. Dualistic religion, with its threat of hell and damnation, is especially coercive. These parents are willing to damn their own children rather than tolerate any differences.

I once knew a man whose gay teenage son came out of the closet. At first, his father refused to believe his son was gay. He insisted that since he himself wasn't gay, his son couldn't be gay. Several weeks later, he overheard his son talking on the phone with his boyfriend. Unable to deny his son's homosexuality any longer, he threw him out. When he related the story to me, I told him his treatment of his son wasn't loving. He said, "How could I permit *that* in my home?" In one fell swoop, his son had gone from being his beloved child to a *that,* a nonperson meriting rejection. When his son was no longer a copy of himself, he had no value.

Fortunately, my parents gave me the gift of autonomy. They loved me enough to allow me to live my own life. They watched from a distance and yet were there when I needed them. They set boundaries, punished gently, but never allowed my behavior to diminish their love. The respect they gave me enabled me to respect my children. More important, it was crucial in helping me imagine a God who respects his children as well.

Giving up control of my children was a spiritual and emotional challenge. When my daughter was ten, she developed a large growth on her neck. The pediatrician took one look and sent us to a specialist. The specialist saw us over his lunch hour and immediately sent us to the hospital. She was in surgery the next day. From the repeated questions of the doctors, we knew they suspected cancer.

As my wife and I sat in the waiting room, I found myself praying as never before. I pleaded with God to save my daughter. In the midst of my struggle, I realized God loved her more than I did. This assurance brought me peace. I could trust her to God's hands. Whether she lived or died, she would be well. I rejoiced nearly as much in this hope as I did when the doctor announced the tumor was benign.

It is when we believe God loves our children less than we do that we fear for their safety. If God loves them as much as we do, they are safe even in the face of death. Their eternal destiny is secure. We no longer have to save our children.

Dualistic theology creates considerable parental anxiety. What if my child is spiritually lost? Such fear causes even the best of parents to meddle in their children's lives. We can easily slip from encouraging our children's spiritual exploration into demanding religious adherence. Only when I abandoned a dualistic theology was I finally free to relate to my children without fear or anxiety. I could encourage and advise, but cease my efforts to manipulate or control. (Well, at least not as often.)

God has no grandchildren. My children cannot inherit my faith. I can't save them. Each of us is on a journey. My role as a parent is not to convert my children, but to live a life consistent with my experience of God's radical love and trust that such a life will attract them. I do this knowing most teenagers rebel and experiment. They test the boundaries. I do this realizing the paths my children choose may not be mine. My response to their choices is not to panic or control, but to love them unconditionally, as God loves me.

As with my wife, I'm learning to respect my children as spiritual beings capable of teaching me. Years ago, when I was struggling with my opinion on homosexuality, the topic came up at our dinner table. My ten-year-old daughter asked what I thought. I explained what I'd been taught—that homosexuality was a sin—and admitted my uncertainty. My daughter said, "I don't think God cares about who you love as long as you love somebody." My daughter's words touched me deeply. I'd been struggling with sexuality when I could have been focusing on human need and the divine call to love.

Grace begins at home. One gift we give to the world is homes full of grace and acceptance, where spouses and children can learn from and teach one another. The world cannot be seriously altered until our homes become incubators, giving birth to a new way of living together. When children are raised in gracious homes, they will be equipped to work and play graciously in the world.

Working Graciously

I remember when Howard Hughes died in 1976. It wasn't because I'd followed his career, admired his movies, or been intrigued by his eccentricity. It was because I heard a sermon with Howard Hughes as the chief illustration.

The preacher detailed Hughes's remarkable life, his wealth, movies, playboy reputation, and fame. Repeatedly, he reminded us of the many ways Hughes had violated the commandments, ignored God, and lived a reprobate life. Clearly, though Hughes had been successful, he had not been a good Christian. The finale of this twisted biography was the preacher's suggestion for the epitaph on Hughes's tombstone: "What shall it profit a man if he shall gain the whole world, and lose his own soul?" (Mark 8:36, KJV). Then, lest we become eccentric playboy billionaire hermits, we were invited to the altar.

Years later, I discovered this sermon formula is an evangelical favorite. Whenever a famous sinner died, preachers across the nation ridiculed their vanity and consigned them to the flames of hell. Whatever they accomplished, however admirable, was irrelevant. They had wasted their lives.

When I believed that some would be saved and others would be damned, I found comfort in such sermons. They implied that those who were successful in this world had mistaken the purpose of life, that in the end we humble Christians had the last laugh. But there are many ways to waste one's life. Though living for fame and fortune is spiritually empty, many religious answers are equally barren.

Dualistic theologies reduce the questions of life to one: Are you saved? Nothing else matters. The purpose of life is to answer that single question. Of course, simply saying "yes" isn't enough. You confirm your salvation by accepting Jesus as Lord and Savior, getting baptized, and receiving the Holy Spirit. Until you have done these things, your life has no meaning.

When salvation is defined so narrowly, it too easily becomes a status rather than a process. It becomes a contractual agreement between an individual and God. Preachers in my childhood often invited us to the altar to "do business with God." We were taught the four spiritual laws. We admitted we were sinners, repented, accepted Jesus, and in return received a nonrefundable reservation in heaven and certain fringe benefits on earth. Too often, God's desire to transform us into mature, responsible, and gracious people was obscured. When religion factored in the fragility of life and the threat of eternal damnation, the product (a spot in heaven) rather than the process (becoming an authentic person) became the priority.

Growing up, I was asked repeatedly, "If you were to die tonight, where would you spend eternity?" I was never asked, "If you live tomorrow, what kind of life will it be?"

Once we were saved, our primary task was to save others. As teens, we were trained to share the four spiritual laws—the religious equivalent of the Heimlich maneuver. We were told that, if followed sincerely, this formula could save a person instantly. We were taught exponential evangelism—if I saved two persons, they each saved two persons, and then they each saved two persons, the whole world would be saved in three years. You can imagine my dismay when I labored to save two people and three years later the world wasn't converted to Christianity. Someone had obviously fallen down on the job.

Saving others was the chief purpose of life. I remember how, during the final worship service at camp, teenager after teenager would stand to proclaim their new commitment to God. The boys would talk of becoming preachers. The girls would pledge to become pastors' wives or missionaries. (It was acceptable for women to preach to African and Asian men.) I never remember anyone's promising to become a gracious banker, police officer, doctor, or lawyer.

Working to make the world a more gracious place wasn't a priority in the churches of my childhood. Some of this negligence was a result of apocalyptic interpretations in which the world was doomed and damned anyway. One man insisted we shouldn't work for peace in the Middle East because we were simply postponing Armageddon and the return of Christ. However, the primary reason the church didn't have time to change the world was because we'd expended so much energy trying to save souls. We'd work for weeks on revivals, evangelism programs, mission support, and the like. We didn't have time for soup kitchens, visiting prisoners, or working with the homeless—unless, of course, we could figure out a way to work in an altar call.

When I became convinced of God's intention to save every person, my perspective on the purpose of life changed. Salvation became as a lifelong adventure in which God is gently and patiently drawing us away from self-absorption and toward authentic relationship with God and one another. The point of life was no longer to get saved or to save others. The purpose of life was to live graciously. Freed from personal anxiety about God's acceptance and no longer obsessed with creating others in my own image, I was able to focus on what it means to *be* rather than *do*.

I remember what my father said when, in the months before college, I asked him what I should do with my life. He answered, "I'm not so worried about what you do with your life. My concern is the kind of person you'll be." At the time, I'd thought his response less than helpful. It took many years to appreciate the wisdom of his counsel.

Our vocation matters, but what is far more important is the person we *are* in our work. Religious vocations aren't confined to churches, synagogues, or mosques. Indeed, those working in what we call secular occupations are often in the best positions to minister to troubled minds and hungry hearts. When I was a Little League coach, I had far more opportunities to serve others than when sitting in my church office. No one need become a pastor, priest, nun, or monk in order to dedicate one's life to God. What the world needs is people *being* gracious wherever they work.

Saving souls isn't about altar calls, but about responding graciously to those we encounter in our daily lives. Being gracious is not about inviting others to church, but about living an inviting life—one both attractive and winsome. The purpose of life isn't to create more Christians, but "to let our lights shine before others, so they will see our good works and give glory to our Father in heaven" (Matthew 5:16).

Having said all of that, there are occupations we should probably abandon. Work that inherently diminishes our worth or the worth of others should be avoided. I encouraged the woman in our church who was dancing in a club to seek other employment. I've also asked people employed in manufacturing bombs and tanks to reconsider their vocation. I did this gently, aware of the economic realities that often place people in such positions and conscious of how my education and affluence make such ethical distinctions easier for me. It is difficult, in an ungracious world, for many to find a place where *doing* and *being* can unite.

In his book *Beyond Words,* Frederick Buechner writes, "The kind of work God usually calls you to is the kind of work (a) that you need most to do and (b) that the world most needs to have done."[3] Much of the unhappiness we experience at work is because we're not doing what fills us with joy and the world with goodness. This misery is obvious in many low-status jobs, but it also plagues boardrooms.

We will inevitably be miserable, no matter how high the salary, exalted the title, or generous the benefits, if we are not doing something that makes the world a more gracious place.

Tony Campolo, a Christian activist, tells the story of the young college student he took on a mission trip to Haiti. They toured that impoverished land, worked in its clinics, taught in its schools, spent long evenings talking with its people. At the end of the trip, the young man promised Tony that he was going to go to medical school and some-day return to Haiti.

Years later, Tony was speaking in a city and ran into this former student on the street. Tony threw his arms around him and asked him how he was. The man was strangely re-served.

Tony asked, "How are you? Did you go to med school? Did you become a doctor?"

The man answered, "Yes, I did."

Tony said, "Wonderful. What's your specialty?"

The man hesitated. "I'm a plastic surgeon."

Tony said, "It must be exciting to heal burn victims and disabled children."

Reluctantly, the man admitted his specialty was cos-metic surgery for rich socialites. He had never returned to Haiti.

Tony follows that story with the story of another young college student—bright, African American, prelaw. He grad-uated from college and then law school with the highest honors. He was recruited to serve as an assistant to the U.S. Supreme Court—the fast track to power and prestige. But he turned it all down. Instead, he decided to represent poor men and women on Georgia's death row. There isn't much money or prestige in that. He lives in a small efficiency apartment. He works long hours and often, in the end, his clients are still executed.

Tony Campolo explains the difference between these two men with these words: "To be full of the Spirit is to have your heart broken by the things that break the heart of God." To be miserable is to exchange the joy of healing the brokenhearted, whether as a doctor, lawyer, waitress, or janitor, for baubles and beads.

This doesn't mean we all have to become inner-city lawyers or missionaries to Haiti. We must find that place of joy for both us and the world. Buechner wrote:

> If you really get a kick out of your work, you've met requirement (a), but if your work is writing cigarette ads, the chances are you've missed requirement (b). On the other hand, if your work is being a doctor in a leper colony, you've probably met requirement (b), but if most of the time you're bored and depressed by it, the chances are you have not only bypassed (a), but probably aren't helping your patients much either. Neither the hair shirt nor the soft berth will do. The place God calls you to is where your deep gladness and the world's deep hunger meet.[4]

Of course, the deepest gladness comes when we realize that the world's deepest hunger is for men and woman who approach every task in life with grace and joy. In the end, when we've finally been humbled by God's love for us and inspired to love others with this same exuberance, living graciously in any and every situation becomes a possibility.

Brother Lawrence of the Resurrection, a seventeenth-century French monk who spent most of his life cleaning pots and pans, managed to bring to that task a mindfulness of spirit he called "practicing the presence of God." He said, "We ought not to be weary of doing little things for the love of God, who regards not the greatness of the work, but the love with which it is performed."[5] We all begin by seeking gracious work, but with maturity comes the ability to work graciously.

Several years ago, I read an article about Henri Nouwen, a Catholic monk and renowned writer. Toward the end of his life, Nouwen had become overwhelmed by a busy speaking and writing career. Trying to maintain his spiritual center, he served in a Canadian monastery that cared for severely handicapped persons.

When the reporter went to interview Nouwen, he asked the receptionist where he could find the famous man. He was directed down a hallway to the third door on the left. He expected to find Nouwen in some cloistered office piled high with books or gently ministering to the needs of some poor, afflicted soul. When he arrived at the third door on the left, he pushed it open to find himself in a public bathroom. Certain he'd misunderstood his directions, he asked the janitor, a little man who was whistling while he scrubbed toilets, if he could direct him to Henri Nouwen. The man looked up and said, "You've found him."

Do you want to make a difference in this world? Do you want the work of your hands to bring gladness, to have meaning and purpose? Do you want your gifts and efforts to meet the world's deep hunger, for your work to be the cause of much joy? Most of all, do you want to learn what Henri Nouwen had learned—how to find joy even in cleaning a toilet?

How I wish this was the altar call of the Church. How I wish, rather than teaching people how to invite others to church or save them in four easy steps, we were encouraging men and women in every walk of life to see themselves as partners in God's grand and gracious work in the world. It is time to be the salt, the leaven, and the light—to accept our responsibility to transform our world.

The commitment to live graciously with family and friends and to work for a more gracious world is our true vocation. It is that to which God is calling us, regardless of our situation, occupation, or social status. Whether we are at home, at work, or at play, grace must inform every aspect of our lives.

Playing Graciously

The president of a large corporation was once asked how he chose those to hire and promote. He answered, "I take them to a nice restaurant for dinner and watch how they treat the waiters or waitresses. I observe how they deal with people when they're relaxed. If they treat graciously those who serve them dinner, I know they'll earn the respect and loyalty of those who work with and for them."

How we play matters.

In recent years, many therapists have learned that watching children play can tell much about their thinking and behavior. If children constantly do violence to their dolls, it could suggest they've been the victims of physical abuse. If they refuse to interact with other children or guard their toys jealously, it could indicate serious problems in their home life. Oddly, though we've realized the relevance of examining how children play, we've largely ignored the lessons of adult play.

When I was young adult, I was an extremely competitive person. Since I was never a great athlete, I competed in the academic arena. I measured myself against others by the grades I received and the awards I won. I reveled in beating others in the games of the mind. I, like many, gave my verbal assent to the adage, "It's not important whether you win or lose; it's how you play the game," but I seldom played unless the game could have a winner and loser and I stood a good chance of winning. It wasn't until I accepted God's unconditional love for me and for all others that I recognized how much dualistic religion encouraged such an approach to life.

Paul writes: "Do you not know that in a race the runners compete, but only one receives the prize? Run in such a way that you may win it" (1 Corinthians 9:24). Unfortunately, Paul's words reflect a common theme in religion—there are a limited number of prizes. This assumption permeates the Bible, from Israel's insistence on being chosen over the other nations to the Christian assertion that only we'll be saved. Religion becomes one more arena of competition, though in religion the game is high stakes—the winners gain paradise and the losers are damned.

It is little wonder those trained to understand the spiritual life as a competition would transfer that same distortion to the rest of life. In dualistic systems, there has to be a winner and a loser—someone saved and someone damned. Indeed, often when I speak of universal salvation, someone will ask, "If everyone is going to be saved, what's the point?" The thought that everyone might be a winner is disturbing to those who've been trained that winning the prize is the point.

This is a difficult idea to abandon. For many years, I led an annual summer youth program. At the beginning of the program, we placed the teenagers in teams of four and ran them through an obstacle course. Before they began, we tied one person's hands in back, tied another's feet together, blindfolded one, and told another to walk backward. We told them they would be competing with the other teams. What we didn't tell them was the criteria for success.

Without fail, each team would hurry through the obstacle course and leave the blindfolded person far behind. Indeed, the others would arrive at the end of course and only then yell their encouragement or derision at their teammate. They were so completely focused on their success, they were willing to leave someone else behind. When all the teams had finished the course, we'd announce that they'd all lost, that the goal was to arrive at the finish line together. In ten years of doing this exercise, we never had a team finish together.

We've been trained to see one another as competitors rather than teammates. I'm not sure whether self-interest caused us to create competitive religion, or whether dualistic religions encouraged self-interest. Regardless, many of us assume our eternal destiny is determined in a cosmic game with winners and losers. We seldom consider the possibility that God wants all of us to cross the finish line together.

Our play often reflects our basic assumptions about life. Living graciously requires us to play differently. No longer are we obsessed with winning. We seek those activities that connect us with rather than divide us from one another. Our play no longer seeks to dominate or defeat, but to enhance our relationships with others. Friendly competition is still possible, but the point is to strengthen our friendships. Play becomes one more means of creating a more gracious world.

When I was a boy I had a gym teacher who never allowed us to pick teams or play competitive games. She'd teach us games like earth ball, in which everyone was on the same team. She'd gather us together at one end of the gym, place the earth ball on top of our outstretched hands, and tell us our goal was to get the ball from one end of the gym to the other without letting it fall to the floor.

This was tougher than you'd think. The ball was so large it took several of us to lift it into the air. We'd have to coordinate our movements to bounce it in the air again. The task was made harder because it went against the grain. The most competitive among us would push it forward too hard and it would hit the floor before we scrambled underneath it. Only when we worked together, moving as a team that included everyone, could we move the earth ball from one end of the gym to the other.

Naturally, I hated the game.

I suspect the game was a parable. We were all one team, we'd all been chosen. No one was left standing against the wall. Our task was to move the earth—a simple task if we worked together as a team, an impossible task if we insisted on competing with each other. We needed everyone, the athlete and the bookworm, the prom queen and the nerd, the first and the last. Everyone played, and everyone was a winner.

Thirty years later, I'm finally allowing the lessons of such games to inform my theology. Life isn't about assuring my own destiny while leaving those with greater handicaps behind. It isn't about different religious teams competing for a single prize. A theology of universal grace is a theology in which everyone eventually wins. Our task is to help the blind and lame to the finish line. Just as faith ought to inform our work, so also should it inform our play.

Initially, I thought the salvation of all people a theological idea. Eventually, I discovered its application to my family and work. Only recently have I considered its implications for my every behavior. What do I watch on television? What movies do I attend? What games do I play or watch? How do I spend my leisure time? I won't pretend to have to answer for every situation or person. However, I am convinced that any activity that reminds us of our connectedness and inspires our acceptance of one another is an act of grace. Any game or pastime that divides us contributes to the dysfunction of our world.

I grew up watching westerns and war movies, playing with toy guns and conquering the world on a Risk game board. Though I eventually became a pacifist, I found it difficult to leave these pastimes behind. I'd protest against war and yet attend movies that glorified military valor. I'd teach my children not to hit, then rent *The Karate Kid* for them to view. I complained how the violence on television impacted my children, but pretended it had no effect on me. More worrisome, I ridiculed movies that celebrated relationship as "chick flicks."

One day I read, "Whatever is true, whatever is honorable, whatever is just, whatever is pure, whatever is pleasing, whatever is commendable, if there is any excellence and if there is anything worthy of praise, think about these things" (Philippians 4:8). I realized I could no longer pretend what I did with my leisure time was irrelevant. Indeed, I began to suspect it is as reflective of my spiritual maturity as any arena of life.

I've reached the age of my life when I've begun to actually think about retirement. There was a time when I dreamed of traveling, playing golf, and finally being able to focus all my time and attention on myself. Though I can certainly understand the need to slow down and refocus our energies as we age, I fear many of our visions of retirement are celebrations of self-absorption. The mature spiritual life doesn't culminate in the purchase of a recreational vehicle.

In fact, the happiest retirees I know are those men and women who've devoted their later years to bettering the world. They gather food and clothing for the poor, they urge political leaders to use their power for good and noble ends, they mentor youth, they volunteer in hospices and hospitals, soup kitchens and schools. They joke often about having no time for retirement, that they are too busy. Yet filling their leisure with gracious activity has infused their lives with joy and meaning.

Living graciously at home, work, and play is the greatest challenge of life. The measure of grace isn't in the creeds I affirm or my behavior on Sunday morning. Grace is proven when I take the time to listen to my wife share her excitement about a hobby I don't find especially interesting, or how I handle the first time my child says, "I hate you," or how I respond when my boss vents his frustration on me, or how I treat the waitress who serves me. Jesus said, "No good tree bears bad fruit, nor again does a bad tree bear good fruit; for each tree is known by its own fruit" (Luke 6:43–44). Those transformed by the grace of God are known by their gracious life.

Sadly, the religious life and the gracious life are often at odds. Many churches, synagogues, and mosques, rather than being orchards of trees bursting with fruit, have been barren wastelands where grace is diminished, if not opposed. Instead of being encouraged to produce fruit, we've been trained to be fruit inspectors. We've been so busy building walls around our particular orchards that we haven't realized how ugly, gnarled, and unproductive they've become. Religion, rather than being a gracious force in the world, has been part of the problem.

1. Thomas Merton, *No Man Is an Island* (New York: Harcourt Brace Jovanovich, 1955), p. 9. Merton diagnoses many of the deep spiritual diseases of our day in this set of essays. Fortunately, he also offers treatment.
2. Dan Brown, *The Da Vinci Code* (New York: Doubleday, 2003).
3. Frederick Buechner, *Beyond Words* (San Francisco: HarperSanFrancisco, 2004), p. 404. This book is full of wonderful insights on a myriad of topics.
4. Buechner, *Beyond Words,* pp. 404–5.
5. Brother Lawrence, *The Practice of the Presence of God* (Old Tappan, NJ: Revell, 1967), p. 27. Brother Lawrence, who passed on his wisdom in a series of conversations and letters, reminds modern readers how to center our lives in God.

5

Gracious Religion

A little girl, her mother, and grandmother were driving home from church one night, after watching a Christian movie about the end of the world, when five-year-old Stacy, who'd been unusually quiet, piped up from the backseat, "I want to ask Jesus into my heart." Her mother and grandmother, sitting in the front seat, instead of questioning why a five-year-old suddenly wanted to "accept Jesus," were overjoyed.

Stacy's mother and grandmother were unconcerned that her decision came after watching a movie that threatened terrible consequences for all those who hadn't accepted Jesus. They didn't question whether Stacy, at the age of five, could comprehend the complexities of committing herself to a religious faith. That night, after some discussion, they led little Stacy in a prayer in which she accepted Jesus as Lord and Savior.

When her grandmother shared this news with me, she admitted some embarrassment. She knew fear had played a part in Stacy's decision. Unfortunately, her relief in knowing Stacy's destiny was secure was greater than her shame at the circumstances. Since the point of her religion was to get people saved, she was pleased.

I understand her delight. In traditional Christianity, our children and grandchildren are damned if they die without meeting the prerequisites of salvation. This assumption worries many parents. Some traditions have responded to this anxiety with infant baptism. Others, insisting on informed consent, have posited an age of innocence during which children aren't accountable for their sins. Since no one seems able to determine precisely when this age ends, there is considerable pressure to convert children as early as possible. Good parents want to do all in their power to assure their children's eternal security. For many parents, getting their children saved is their highest priority.

This is the problem with fear-based and heaven-earning religion—any means, no matter how manipulative, to convert your children is justifiable. Since I've already paid considerable attention to the inadequacies of a religion or a relationship based on such motives, I won't belabor the point. What I find more interesting is what happened on the Monday morning after Stacy accepted Jesus into her heart.

The next day, Stacy, less somber and more mischievous, misbehaved. Her mother said, "You know, Stacy, a little girl who asked Jesus into her heart shouldn't act that way."

Stacy replied, "Well, I can ask him out too."

When Stacy's grandmother told me this story, she suggested Stacy had figured out the nature of the universe—you can choose to accept or reject God. I doubt five-year-olds give much thought to the nature of the universe. They are, however, sensitive to fear and resistant to control. Stacy discovered at an early age how often religion resorts to such mechanisms.

Karl Marx would have appreciated Stacy's retort. He argued religion was the "opium of the people." It was a means for the elite to control and pacify the poor and oppressed. Marx suggested Christianity's unwillingness to adopt the social ethic of Jesus was a clear indication of religion's true motive—the desire to control and oppress. Though communism proved as vulnerable to this corruption as religion, his criticism remains accurate.

For many, religion is a means of controlling human behavior. Dualistic religion, with the threat of hell and the offer of heaven, is especially susceptible to this temptation. Pain and pleasure, the two primary human stimulants, become the tools of salvation. Unfortunately, the reliance of religion on such primal instincts ignores those faculties that elevate humans from the animal kingdom—our ability to endure pain and forgo pleasure in the pursuit of what is good and noble. Ironically, when we reduce religion to a controlling mechanism, we often create humans with little self-control.

A mother, after hearing me speak on God's universal grace, complained, "Don't be telling my son that everyone will be saved. It's taken me years to put the fear of God in him, and I don't want him going crazy now." Sadly, we soon learned her son had been involved in some sexually deviant behavior. Fear had not produced the control she had hoped for. Her son, having been manipulated by the threat of pain and offer of pleasure, was unable to discover any higher motive for his life.

I saw this dynamic often in the conservative Christian college I attended, where we had to sign a lifestyle statement pledging to not drink, smoke, dance, or be sexually active during our four years of college. Those who'd been most tightly controlled during their upbringing were the first to self-destruct when given the least bit of freedom. When these students were expelled, their parents often blamed the college for being too permissive.

The problem with controlling religion is that it is so convinced of the depravity of humanity that it cannot believe anyone could live a good life without manipulation or coercion. The moral atheist is a mystery to many religious people. It was no mystery to Jesus. He thought goodness the product of an internal commitment and not an external demand. He said, "The good person out of the good treasure of the heart produces good, and the evil person out of evil treasure produces evil" (Luke 6:45).

To extend Jesus's metaphor, goodness is rooted in a commitment to love others. Those who love are good; those who are good, love. In my experience, this quality is not limited to Christians, or even the religious. Wherever compassion occurs, God is present, willing to be anonymous as long as his children are being loved. Goodness is never about controlling others, but about loving them.

Jesus turns controlling religion, with its inflexible laws and requirements, on its head. The point isn't obeying the rules (an act of the will), but in producing good fruit (an overflow of the heart). Our hearts are changed only when we realize God's unconditional love for us and embrace our responsibility to love others unconditionally. We don't need to accept Jesus into our hearts; we need to have the same heart as Jesus.

When five-year-old Stacy said, "Well, I can ask him out too," she wasn't rejecting the life and message of Jesus. She was rejecting a type of religion meant to control rather than encourage. I think she made the right choice. She recognized a lack of grace. She was willing to say at five what I couldn't say until I was thirty-five—if that's what religion is, I want nothing to do with it.

This is why many have left the church, synagogue, and mosque. They aren't atheists. They've simply found the courage to reject religious fear and control. They seek a spirituality consistent with what they sense to be true— there must be more to life than escaping hell and keeping the rules. They yearn for a way of life that is gentle, humble, open, and compassionate.

Gentle Religion

In *Traveling Mercies: Some Thoughts on Faith,* Anne Lamott tells of her conversion to Christianity. After many years of spiritual wandering and self-destructive behavior, she found herself attending a small Presbyterian church. "I went back to St. Andrew about once a month. No one tried to con me into sitting down or staying. I always left before the sermon. I loved singing, even about Jesus, but I didn't want to be preached at about him."

At the same time, Lamott's life was a mess. Her dearest friend was dying of cancer. She was despondent following an abortion. She spent many days in a drugged and alcoholic stupor. In the midst of her deep depression, she describes a presence—something like having a cat watching her. "I felt him sitting there on his haunches in the corner of my sleeping loft, watching me with patience and love, and I squinched my eyes shut, but that didn't help because that's not what I was seeing him with."

One week later, Lamott was sitting at St. Andrew when the singing touched a chord deep within her. "I began to cry and left before the benediction, and I raced home and felt the little cat running along at my heels, and I walked down the dock past dozens of potted flowers, under a sky as blue as one of God's own dreams, and I opened the door of my houseboat, and I stood there a minute, and I hung my head and said, 'Fuck it: I quit.' I took a long deep breath and said out loud, 'All right. You can come in.'"[1]

In the churches I grew up in, people would have been so offended by Lamott's language they'd have missed the beauty of her description of God. The God she experienced was gently persistent—waiting patiently for her response and loving her too much to violate her autonomy. Fortunately, the church Lamott was attending was equally gracious, giving her space to wrestle with God.

I'm glad Anne Lamott didn't attend my first church. I'd been taught to pursue the reluctant, resistant, and lost. I contacted people within twenty-four hours of their first visit. I'd barge into their homes, interrogate them about their spiritual status, and imply they needed to get right with God. If they missed a Sunday, I'd hunt them down and ask what was wrong. If Lamott had shared her struggles, I would have been quick to offer platitudes and assurances. I was an aggressive Christian—more like a pit bull than a kitten.

If you'd asked me what motivated my behavior, I would have claimed a deep concern for saving the lost. In retrospect, I realize my motives weren't always so pure. It was my first pastorate and, like any person in a new career, I wanted to be successful. I counted every person who attended worship each Sunday. When the numbers were up, I was happy. When attendance was down, I was depressed. My ministry, even when it spoke of God's grace, wasn't always gracious. I wanted people to join "my" church, adopt my beliefs, conform to my expectations, and do this as quickly as possible. My ministry was often selfish, aggressive, and ungracious.

Gracious religion is gentle, making room for a person to mature, knowing this takes time and often comes with pain and struggle. It is not impatient or intrusive. It respects the integrity of the other person too much to coerce or manipulate. Gracious religion is convinced that in the end every person will recognize the truth—that we are loved and created to love. We shall all know this truth, and this truth shall set us free. When by word or action we resist this truth, God waits patiently. When we finally end our rebellion, God's joy is full.

The great religions, at their best, recognize the need for this gentleness. The Qur'an says, "Let there be no compulsion in religion" (2:257). This verse inspired Islam to be tolerant. Historically, Muslims respected the rights and practices of Jews and Christians far more than those communities respected them. This tolerance was the result of two assumptions, one being that, though Muhammad was the last great prophet, God had revealed God's self through others—Abraham, Moses, and Jesus. More important, the Prophet taught that belief is a gift of God. Forcing someone to believe in God is a contradiction. The beliefs that transform our lives resonate within us. The truth may be proclaimed to us, but we believe only when the proclamation stirs something deep within us.

Buddha taught, "Do not accept what you hear by report, do not accept tradition, do not accept a statement because it is found in our books, nor because it is in accord with your belief, nor because it is the saying of your teacher. Be lamps unto yourselves."[2] This is remarkably close to Jesus's proclamation that "the kingdom of God is within you" (Luke 17:21). Both men were convinced the truth was less a matter of external seeking and more about internal revelation. Truth is not given to us by religion. Gracious religion helps us to discover what is true. It does this gently.

Jesus never led an altar call. He didn't baptize anyone. He didn't take the woman at the well through the four spiritual laws. Most of what Christianity calls evangelism would be alien to Jesus. He told stories. In one story, he described his approach as scattering seed. He recognized much of that seed would fall on hard ground, but where the soil was ready, the seed would take root.

Paul, building on this metaphor, reminds Christians they might plant and water, but "only God gives the growth" (1 Corinthians 3:7). Early in my ministry, I was a poor gardener. I planted one day and wanted to harvest the next. When I didn't see immediate results, I'd dig up the seed to see what was wrong. I didn't allow different people to grow at different paces. I didn't adjust my watering for different needs. I treated the cactus like the willow. I was quick to rip up both the wheat and the tares. Gently, God taught me to slow down and watch the miracle of growth— given time and a little encouragement, everything grows.

Dualistic theologies tend to be impatient. Judgment and condemnation await those who dally. God's grace ends at the grave. This race with death makes it easy to justify nearly any shortcut or manipulation. Only when we grasp that religion should help us grow can we lay down the weapons of coercion and control.

No one can discern the truth, let alone fully and freely embrace it, while under the threat of hell. People cannot grow into authentic human beings if their religious communities control their every experience and idea. People cannot come to an authentic faith if their beliefs are the result of indoctrination rather than revelation. Even the Amish, who demand and enforce rigid conformity, have a practice called *rumspringa,* during which their teenagers are permitted to experience the outside world. The assumption is that, if the Amish way of life is compelling, the teenagers will eventually return.

Of course, they may be wrong. Their children may experience the greater world and decide the beliefs and practices of their childhood faith aren't sufficient. They may discover other ways of living more authentically. Unfortunately, if Amish teens make this decision, they risk being shunned.

Gracious religion never shuns. It offers as much time and space as necessary. It refuses to be shocked by our doubts and questions or scandalized by our resistance. Years ago, a woman in my congregation passed away. Her husband, a once sporadic attendee, began attending worship more frequently. He would often stand during the Quaker silence and preface his remarks by saying, "Now, you should know I don't believe in God anymore, but . . ." and then proceed to share some insight or experience.

When this first happened, I wasn't sure how the congregation would respond. Earlier in my ministry, I would have cringed, then made it my goal to restore him to faith. Instead, I watched the congregation, who seemed at ease with his admission, continue to care for him in his grief.

One day, after worship, I asked him why he continued to attend church if he no longer believed in God. I wasn't trying to be argumentative. I was more curious than anything. He replied, "Because when I leave here, I feel better than when I arrived. These people love me."

Over the next several years, as he continued to share his misgivings, I never heard anyone in the congregation criticize or berate him for his atheism. Indeed, one of the saints of the church would often reply, "I can understand how you would feel that way."

Slowly, over a period of three years, his faith reemerged. Not because any of us demanded it, but because time was allowed for the leavening effect of grace. Had we insisted on a premature and dramatic return to faith, I believe he would have been lost to us and further estranged from God.

This is what it means to love others as God loves them, to be willing to patiently and gently await that day, in this life or the next, when grace is triumphant. Until that day, gracious religion must help people feel better—more fully loved, more fully human—when they leave than when they arrived. We embrace them not just when their faith is strong, but especially when it isn't. The good news is that even when we run away, God stays close to our heels, like Anne Lamott's little cat, anticipating the day we'll open the door.

Humble Religion

A father brought his epileptic child to Jesus to be healed. He said, "If you are able to do anything, have pity on us and help us." Jesus replied, "If you are able!—All things can be done for the one who believes." Immediately, the father of the child cried out, "I believe; help my unbelief!" (Mark 9:22–24). I love the honesty and humility of that answer.

The religion of my childhood encouraged neither of these qualities. Questions that challenged the pat answers were viewed as unfaithful. When I asked how Jesus could be both divine and human, I was told it was a mystery. It couldn't be explained, but must be accepted. The faithful believed the illogical, impossible, and irrational. Doubts, if we had any, were best kept to ourselves. Unbelievers were doomed to hell. Jesus was the answer. Christianity was the only way. We possessed the whole truth. Our task was to correct, convince, or coerce others. We were encouraged to begin with our own families. In the midst of this enthusiasm, I decided to save my aunt Nancy.

Nancy was a wonderful woman, intelligent, vivacious, and caring. She was a loved and respected junior-high teacher. Her students would return years later to thank her for her compassion. I experienced this care each year when she hosted our family for Thanksgiving. Going to her house and being with her was one of the highlights of each year. My only discomfort was that she'd quit attending church during college. Though she often spoke of spiritual matters, her opinion of Christianity was low.

One year, after returning home from Thanksgiving, I decided to write my aunt. I shared my experience with God, discussed my beliefs, and asked her to accept Jesus as Lord and Savior. I told her I was motivated out of concern for her, the quality of her life, and her eternal destiny. I prayed over the letter and asked God to reveal the truth.

Several weeks later I received her reply in the mail. It was not the answer I'd hoped for, but it was precisely what I needed. She spoke of her own spiritual journey, of how she had experienced and known God, of what she'd rejected as inauthentic, and of the peace she'd finally discovered. Then she challenged my motives. She suggested my concern was not for her, but for myself. What had made me uncomfortable was that she had found peace and meaning in ways different from mine. What concerned me was the possibility that there might be other ways of knowing God.

My prayer was answered. The truth was revealed—not to her, but to me. I realized my arrogance in assuming another human being should relate to God exactly as I did. Gracious religion approaches others gently because, even if our experience is more authentic or accurate than theirs, no one can or should adopt an experience that isn't their own. It approaches others humbly because their experience of

God may be more authentic and accurate than our own. There was nothing wrong with sharing my beliefs and convictions with my aunt Nancy. What was arrogant was my assumption that my faith was more authentic.

Christianity has often been arrogant. Rather than gently waiting on others to come to what we insist is a compelling truth, we demand immediate obedience and conformity. Rather than admitting any possible fallibility, we claim certainty. *Evangelism,* which comes from the Greek word for spreading good news, often degenerates into telling others the bad news—we're saved and you're not.

Christians are not alone in this elitism. All the great religions imply a monopoly on the truth. There is a story that tells of God's placing the totality of all truth in a sphere and asking an angel to deliver the truth to humanity. Unfortunately, while descending, the angel drops the sphere, and it shatters into millions of pieces. The problem is we've each assumed our small piece is the whole truth.

Gandhi said, "It is unwise to be sure of one's own wisdom. It is healthy to be reminded that the strongest might weaken and the wisest might err." I repeat this to myself often as I preach and write. Since I'm not the wisest, I'm certain I err. Reading sermons I preached ten years ago is a good reminder—I passionately proclaimed beliefs I no longer hold. I'm learning to offer my insights and beliefs with humility. I could be wrong.

I'm often asked if I know, without a shadow of a doubt, that all will be saved. The answer is no. When I admit this, some ask, "How can you teach something that might not be true? Don't you worry that you may be leading some astray?" I understand the question. Once I would have asked it myself. The problem with the question is the implication: there are some beliefs about the afterlife, or any other idea for that matter, that can be known beyond the shadow of a doubt.

What happens after death is a mystery. Every belief is speculation. Some people, based on their confidence in the Bible, believe some will go to heaven and others will go to hell. Others, based on their trust in the teachings of the Church, offer the possibility of purgatory. Still others believe, based on their convictions, that we will be reincarnated, or assimilated, or annihilated. The Mormons, if I understand them correctly, believe we'll someday be gods of our own planets.

These are all beliefs. They are not scientific facts we can prove in a laboratory. This doesn't mean we should (or can) abandon speculation. The problem is when we insist our beliefs are the complete truth. This arrogant religion exalts itself and its adherents. As Marcus Borg notes in *The Heart of Christianity:* "When we think about the claim that Christianity is the only way of salvation, it's a pretty strange notion. Does it make sense that [God], whom we speak of as creator of the universe, has chosen to be known in only one religious tradition, which just fortunately happens to be our own?"[3]

Gracious religion, in contrast, adopts an attitude of epistemological humility. It says, "I know, but I could be wrong." This is the paradox of experiences with God—they are the most real and powerful experiences of life, capable of transforming and changing us. Yet they are also intensely personal, difficult to verify, and therefore subject to human limitations and misinterpretations. Though we should be passionate about our religious faith, we do well to remember the words of this Hindu prayer:

> *O Lord, forgive three sins that are due to my human*
>   *limitations:*
> *Thou art everywhere, but I worship you here;*
> *Thou art without form, but I worship you in these forms;*
> *Thou needest no praise, yet I offer these prayers and*
>   *salutations.*
> *Lord, forgive three sins that are due to my human*
>   *limitations.*[4]

I encounter this same humility in the popular Easter hymn "He Lives." Alfred Ackley wrote of his belief in a risen Jesus, alive in the world today. Yet he ended each chorus with the admission, "You ask me how I know he lives? He lives within my heart." The proof is not in archaeological research, DNA testing of the Shroud of Turin, or in proving the reliability of resurrection accounts in the Bible. The truth of any experience is whether it changes our hearts. Are we transformed into more gracious people?

When the passion of our hearts is balanced by an awareness of our limitations, we will live graciously. Accepting our inability to fully communicate what we've experienced and aware of our resistance prior to such experiences, we will not insist on conformity, but offer our insights humbly. We will offer our sliver of the truth even as we appreciate what others have to say.

Open Religion

I grew up in a small Midwestern town where most everyone was white and middle class. My high school had only a handful of minorities and that included Democrats. The churches in our town, although they ascribed to various theological creeds, promoted the same values and behaviors. I attended a Christian college at which our foreign students were either missionary children or converts. Until I was in my twenties, everyone I knew was exactly like me. Those who lived or thought differently than I did were strange.

Growing up, I remember ridiculing the idea of reincarnation. We laughed at the absurdity of Hindus starving because they were afraid a cow might be a grandparent. We wondered why everyone who claimed to be reincarnated was either Cleopatra or Napoleon in a previous life. It was easy to mock what we didn't understand. It was many years before I recognized reincarnation as a serious attempt to explain human destiny, value justice, and deal with the problem of evil and that it was no more fantastic and speculative than claiming the dead rise again. It never occurred to me that my practice of eating the body and drinking the blood of Jesus seemed strange to Hindus.

As I matured, I became curious about others, especially those who were different from me. I wanted to know why someone would believe in reincarnation. I enrolled in a college course on world religions, fully expecting to find my religious views affirmed and the false teachings of other faiths exposed. I was confident Christianity was the only way, truth, and life. On the first day, the professor announced, "All truth is God's truth." He challenged us to approach the beliefs of others with an open mind and heart, to allow whatever truth we encountered, no matter what the source, to transform us.

During the next three months, I encountered God's truth in people and religions I'd previously discounted. As we read the holy writings of Hinduism, Buddhism, Islam, and Judaism, I found myself moved, challenged, and inspired. At the end of the course, though I still thought Christianity superior, I concluded God has been at work in all persons, cultures, and religions.

For the first time in my life, I considered the possibility that people of other cultures and religions might know something important about God that I didn't know. I realized we each know in part and see through the glass dimly. If knowledge and revelation aren't limited to any single person, culture, or religion, we are wise to seek pieces to the puzzle in all people, cultures, and religions.

My experiences over the past twenty-five years have reinforced my sense of God's universal activity, chipping away at my religious elitism. Reading and studying other religions was only the beginning of this transformation. Encountering sincere, intelligent, and passionate men and women holding differing beliefs forced me to take their ideas seriously.

My belief in the salvation of all people began as one such encounter. Sitting around a campfire one night, I listened as a friend explained why he no longer believed God would torture or reject any of his children. My initial response was shock and dismay. Fortunately, the person expressing these views was someone I respected, someone who exemplified the Christian way of life. Though I didn't adopt his belief that night, he provoked my curiosity. Why would a Christian think such a thing?

One of the reasons he gave was his unwillingness to believe God spoke solely to and through one person, culture, or religion. He was suspicious of our tendency to identify our way of imaging and approaching God as the only means of relating to God. He considered compassionate, gracious people of every religion, or of no religion, to share a common commitment—a belief in the worth of all persons. I began to change my mind.

I wasn't the only one changing. Even in my hometown, it has been difficult to ignore the rest of the world. The Islamic Society of North America established its headquarters in our county. Our area experienced an influx of people from others cultures and religions. The Internet made it possible for my neighbors to chat with people on the other side of the world. This ability for people from diverse cultures and belief systems to be in dialogue is as revolutionary today as the printing press was in the Dark Ages. Our shrinking world often produces a broadening of human interaction and wisdom.

Unfortunately, the new and different also produce fear. Many, instead of appreciating and assimilating other beliefs, isolate themselves and resist change at all costs. Some cling to dualistic beliefs as a defense against having to take seriously the experiences and thoughts of others. They reject new ideas as perversion and heresy. They see others as targets for conversion. The rich diversity of our world is a threat rather than a joy.

After a recent lecture, a woman told me, "My pastor announced from the pulpit last night that we were forbidden to come and hear you. I didn't even know you were coming until his announcement, but I knew I had to come and see what was so threatening."

"What do you think?" I asked.

"You're just asking the same questions I've asked."

I doubt this woman will be at her present church much longer. Control and curiosity are ultimately incompatible. Once we ask hard questions and listen to diverse views, we discover those who answer differently aren't the monsters we'd been warned about; they are people like us. They struggle with sin, they seek happiness and meaning, they yearn for relationship with God and others. We begin to hear their religious views as legitimate responses to universal questions.

Being universally curious doesn't mean we'll adopt

every new belief or idea, but neither will we discount them quickly and carelessly. If God loves every person as much as God loves me, God is working in and through others as much as God is at work in and through me. If so, they may know something I need to know. Or they may be as confused as I am. Regardless, I leave open the possibility that God may speak through them to me.

Thich Nhat Hanh, a Buddhist Nobel Peace Prize nominee, writes:

> In a true dialogue, both sides are willing to change. We have to appreciate that truth can be received from outside of—not only within—our own group. If we do not believe that, entering into dialogue would be a waste of time. If we think we monopolize the truth and we still organize a dialogue, it is not authentic. We have to believe that by engaging in dialogue with other persons, we have the possibility of making a change within ourselves, that we can become deeper.[5]

When I was growing up, such dialogue was discouraged. Indeed, young Christians are often warned about speaking with people of different faiths. We weren't to answer the door when the Jehovah's Witnesses or Mormons knocked unless we were mature in the faith. Inflexibility, rather than curiosity, characterized spiritual maturity. I often wondered why, if our views were compelling and their beliefs were false, we didn't welcome discussion. Now I suspect many churches discourage dialogue because of fear. What if someone else has a piece of the truth? Worse yet, what if their worldview proves more helpful than ours? What if they're right and we're wrong?

A lack of curiosity demonstrates our fear and disrespect for others. An easy assurance in our righteousness and right thinking makes it nearly impossible for us to consider any new idea. We become truth keepers rather than truth seekers—quick to speak and slow to listen. This unwillingness to listen to those who think differently is not a sign of faithfulness, but an unwillingness to hear God's messengers. Of course, living in a world of increasing diversity makes ignoring new ideas ever more impossible. The only effective guard against change is to believe your spiritual journey complete.

Our absolute insistence that our way is the only way keeps us from hearing one another. When I first believed God would save all people, I thought God would accomplish this through Jesus Christ. Everyone would eventually, in this life or the next, realize Jesus was the Son of God and accept him as Lord and Savior. The other great religions were wrong, and someday they'd know it.

My study of world religions made such a neat solution troubling. My insistence that all come to God in the way I'd come to God was egotistical and lazy. It allowed me to ignore the rich extent of God's revelation to people in cultures and religions across the world. Religious elitism robbed me of the benefits of God's work in millions of lives. Though I remain a Christian, one who has come to know God through the life and teachings of Jesus, I've accepted my proper place as a seeker after truth rather than the possessor of all wisdom. My curiosity is growing.

Gracious religion isn't an unbending allegiance to a narrow orthodoxy. It is about approaching our life with God and others in a spirit of gentleness, humility, and openness. These tools become the means by which God fits us for citizenship in the world and God's kingdom. It is about being less committed to a rigid, self-concerned institution and more concerned about authenticity, integrity, and faith.

This faith is not about believing the right things about God, but about trusting God to remake us in God's image, full of grace and truth. Its goal is not dogmatic certainty, but making our peace with a great mystery—that God's simple truth is revealed in a multiplicity of forms. All of these forms reflect a common conviction—that we are most like God when we love each other.

Compassionate Religion

"Everyone who loves is born of God and knows God. Whoever does not love does not know God, for God is love" (1 John 4:7–8). It couldn't be clearer. Religion, at its best, encourages and guides us in loving others. The goal is love. Where love is active, the religious rejoice. Where love is absent, they grieve.

One day, the apostle John complained to Jesus, "Master, we saw someone casting out demons in your name, and we tried to stop him, because he does not follow with us." But Jesus said to him, "Do not stop him; for whoever is not against you is for you" (Luke 9:49–50). Jesus was more interested in seeing people made whole and goodness triumph than in maintaining personal authority or control. Unfortunately, John was not the last disciple of Jesus to confuse the issue.

I was once invited to a Baptist conference when I was pastoring a Methodist congregation. One of the speakers discussed the need for church growth. He produced a map of the area and announced that the denomination needed to plant a church in this locale because there were "no churches within a ten-mile radius." Since I knew there were several Methodist churches within his circle, I almost interrupted. Then I realized he meant there were no *Baptist* churches.

I'm not picking on the Baptists. I'm certain in Methodist circles, people often made the same assumption—if we're not ministering there, no ministry is happening. Each group suggests that only those who follow its narrow religious viewpoint are authentic. It sends missionaries to Muslim, Buddhist, and Hindu countries convinced it is the true religion. This is an age-old problem. A story attributed to the Jewish philosopher Moses Mendelssohn illustrates both the seriousness and silliness of this attitude:

A woman once asked the Teacher, "Which is the true religion?"

The Teacher replied, "Once there was a magic ring that gave its bearer the gifts of grace, kindness, and generosity. When the owner of the ring was on his deathbed, each of his three sons came separately and asked him for the ring. The old man promised the ring to each of them.

"He then sent for the finest jeweler in the land and paid him to make two rings identical to the original. The jeweler did so, and before he died, the father gave each son a ring without telling him about the other two.

"Inevitably, the three sons discovered that each one had a ring, and they appeared before the local judge to ask his help in deciding who had the magic ring. The judge examined the rings and found them to be all alike. He then said, 'Why must anyone decide now? We shall know who has the magic ring when we observe the direction your life takes.'

"Each of the brothers then acted as if he had the magic ring by being kind, honest, and thoughtful.

"Now," the Teacher concluded, "religions are like the three brothers in the story. The moment their members cease striving for justice and love we will know that their religion is not the one God gave the world."[6]

Our problem, today as much as in the day of Jesus or Mendelssohn, is that we consider religion a ring to possess rather than a love to express. We are so obsessed with being right that we forget to be gracious. In so doing, we reveal our spiritual immaturity.

I don't believe there are a thousand different paths to God—with one as good as another. I think some religious ideas are abhorrent, others seriously flawed, and none completely satisfactory. This isn't a criticism as much as an acknowledgment that human institutions always mirror human diversity and frailty. This also implies a certain standard by which I judge religious thought and institutions. Does a religious idea or group make the world a more loving place? If so, I don't want to stop it. If not, I don't want to follow it.

For me, the ultimate test is one Jesus suggested. He told

a story of the final judgment. The question on that day was not whether people believed the proper theology, whether they belonged to the One True Church, or whether they'd been baptized in Jesus's name. To the righteous, God simply announced, "When I was hungry and you gave me something to eat, I was thirsty and you gave me something to drink, I was a stranger and you invited me in, I needed clothes and you clothed me, I was sick and you looked after me, I was in prison and you came to visit me." Surprised, many asked, "When did we see you hungry, . . . thirsty, . . . a stranger, . . . needing clothes, . . . sick or in prison?" To which God answered, "Whatever you did for one of the least of these brothers of mine, you did for me" (Matthew 25:34–40, NIV).

When we do such things, we demonstrate the presence of God in our lives. When we act graciously, we leave behind the labels—Christian, Jewish, Muslim, Hindu, Buddhist—that divide us. We claim our proper place as a child of God and a member of the human family.

Confucius said:

When the Great Principle prevails, the world is a Commonwealth in which rulers are selected according to their wisdom and ability. Mutual confidence is promoted and good neighborliness cultivated. Hence, men do not regard as parents only their own parents, nor do they treat as children only their own children. Provision is secured for the aged till death, employment for the able-bodied, and the means of growing up for the young. Helpless widows and widowers, orphans and the lonely, as well as the sick and the disabled, are well cared for.[7]

Gracious religion helps such principles to prevail. It works to create a better world for all. Gracious religion will be gentle, because creating a new world is delicate work. It will be humble, since our visions of this new world will often differ. It will be open, seeking common ground, even as it explores our diversity. Finally, gracious religion will be compassionate, unwilling to leave anyone behind.

Unfortunately, the Christianity of my childhood often lacked these characteristics. It resorted to threats and demands and was impatient with the resistant. It could be arrogant and rude, insisting on its own way. It was tenaciously closed-minded, unwilling to tolerate doubts or questions. It was too exclusive and self-absorbed, comfortable with the damnation of millions. There was a time when I seriously considered Christianity beyond repair.

Today, I am more hopeful. Jesus is one of the reasons. When I examine his life, words, and example, I am profoundly moved. When I take his call to authentic human living seriously, my life is transformed. When I share his confidence in God's ability to redeem even a cross, I no longer despair. Convinced his gracious way of life is the proper way of life, I envision a gracious Christianity—a people committed to being like Jesus.

1. Anne Lamott, *Traveling Mercies: Some Thoughts on Faith* (New York: Pantheon, 1999), p. 47. This spiritual journal is both raw and beautiful— a model for being honest with God and about God.
2. Huston Smith, *The World Religions* (San Francisco: HarperSanFrancisco, 1991), p. 94. This book is one of the great books on comparative religion. Smith makes you want to be an adherent of all the great religions.
3. Marcus Borg, *The Heart of Christianity* (San Francisco: HarperSanFrancisco, 2003), p. 220. A wonderful exploration of what gracious religion might look like.
4. Smith, *World Religions,* p. 34.
5. Thich Nhat Hanh, *Living Buddha, Living Christ* (New York: Riverhead Books, 1995), p. 9. A compelling attempt to assimilate the truths of Christianity with the wisdom of Buddhism.
6. William R. White, *Stories for the Journey* (Minneapolis, MN: Augsburg, 1988), p. 54. This is an anthology of stories and parables from around the world and from within various traditions.
7. David Budbill, "What Confucius Said," *The Judevine Mountain Emailite* (No. 12, April 29, 1999).

6
Gracious Christianity

When I first began writing and speaking about the salvation of all people, I imagined death threats, angry picketers, and auditoriums filled with fierce antagonists crying for my blood. I knew many Christians would find my theology heretical and had read enough Church history to know how Christians treat heretics. Calvin had Servetus burned at the stake for calling Jesus "the eternal Son" rather than "the Son of the Eternal God."

My fears were balanced by satisfaction. I'd been taught persecution was a sign of faithfulness. Having been raised to admire martyrs, I felt an odd attraction to being persecuted for my faith, even if that faith was heretical. I'd discovered the only difference between a martyr and a heretic was who lit the fire. Prepared to suffer, I was surprised to discover far more approval than censure.

There are thousands inside and outside the Church who share my discomfort with the Christianity of our childhood. Many find the proclamation of God's unconditional and eternal love to be good news. They've always thought God capable of such grace, but didn't think they were free to believe it. Many of these people deeply appreciate another view of human destiny. Others, though unable to embrace all my conclusions, have found the discussion intriguing.

Not everyone is a fan. One elderly woman burned my book—light treatment when we remember Servetus. Albert Mohler, a Southern Baptist leader, accused me of telling itching ears what they want to hear. I'm never certain how to answer that charge. I remember all the years I was told people were hungry and thirsty to hear the gospel of Jesus Christ. If we told them the good news, they'd respond. Why is it when people share our beliefs they are wise and spiritually sensitive, but when they are attracted to an idea we oppose they are ignorant and wicked?

I'm as guilty of this prejudice as anyone.

Whenever I speak, I open the floor to questions. Almost always, the first to stand will be someone whose views are diametrically opposed to what I believe, someone who has sat on the edge of the seat impatiently waiting for me to stop talking so I can be put in my place.

"The Bible says Jesus is the way, the truth, and the life and no one comes to the Father except through him. The Bible says believe in the Lord Jesus and you'll be saved. The

Bible says some will be damned and burn in hell for all eternity. Of course, you don't believe the Bible is the Word of God. You pick and choose, only accepting what you like. You don't understand that if one word of the Bible isn't true, then we can't trust any of it. You say everyone is going to be saved. But that's not what the Bible says, Jesus taught, or the Church believes. How can you even call yourself a Christian?"

My initial temptation is to belittle my critic. Even when I resist and respond politely, I often harbor resentment, comforting myself with the thought that the person is either unenlightened and should be pitied or rude and obnoxious and should be ignored. The truth is, like me, such critics are trying to make sense of their faith. They don't need to be patronized or ridiculed, but to be treated graciously. Even if they remain unconvinced, they deserve a careful explanation of what I mean when I call myself a Christian.

It would be easy to spend this chapter recounting all the ways Christianity has failed. There is much about Christianity, past and present, I find troubling. I've considered other faiths, but have encountered the tension between gracious and ungracious living in all of them. In the end, I committed myself to redeeming the faith of my childhood. How can we be both Christian and gracious?

This isn't as easy as you'd think. When measured against the characteristics of gracious religion—gentleness, humility, openness, and compassion—Christianity often falls short. We can be ungracious. Non-Christians are often amazed to discover Jesus taught his followers not to judge. You'd never conclude that from our behavior. We may not burn people at the stake, but we still find a myriad of reasons to exclude and condemn.

Becoming gracious will require a reformation that will make Luther's look like redecorating. It will require us to abandon our claim to be favored children. We'll have to surrender the Bible as our ace in the hole and Jesus as a backstage pass. The Church will have to serve, rather than dominate, the world. Christianity will need to reclaim its most distinctive doctrine—the universal grace of God. Hell and damnation will no longer be tools of the trade. We'll need to identify Christians not by what they believe about Jesus, but by their willingness to be like him.

This is not a new commitment. Gracious Christianity has always existed, though often quietly. Many have tried to live as graciously as Jesus did. They've taken my definition of a Christian—one who follows Jesus—seriously. They've modeled their lives after his life, seeking to be faithful to the biblical witness and their conviction that in a real, though often mysterious way, Jesus lives. Although the language describing his presence has varied widely, they've experienced the Spirit of Jesus drawing them toward God and making them into gracious persons. Like Jesus, they seek to imitate God.

Paul writes, "Therefore be imitators of God, as beloved children, and live in love, as Christ loved us and gave himself up for us, a fragrant offering and sacrifice to God" (Ephesians 5:1–2). The Christianity of my childhood focused much of its thought and energy on the second half of that passage, on celebrating Jesus's sacrifice. We obsessed on John's vision of Jesus as "the Lamb of God who takes away the sin of the world" (John 1:29) and obscured Jesus's consistent call to a life of grace.

Elaine Pagels, in her book *Beyond Belief,* notes, "John's gospel differs from Matthew, Mark and Luke in a second— and far more significant—way, for John suggests that Jesus is not merely God's human servant, but God himself revealed in human form."[1] She argues that the early Church's ideas about Jesus were far more diverse. Many who called Jesus Lord did not limit his work to the cross. Atonement theology, according to which Jesus was born to die and salvation came only in accepting his sacrifice, fought to become the orthodox theology of the Church. Its proponents destroyed, rather than convinced, their opponents.

At the very least, it is time for Christianity to admit that since its earliest days there have been competing definitions of what it means to be Christian. Three of the four Gospels emphasize lifestyle rather than belief. Many early Christians would be scandalized by what we now consider orthodoxy. The definition of heresy has been as fluid as the definition of Christianity.

Today, Protestants and Catholics should be especially aware of theological evolution. How can we ignore the search for truth and relevance that inspired the Reformation and Vatican II? Redefining Christianity isn't heresy, but necessity. This is, and always has been, the case. What I suggest is a form of Christianity that reclaims the first half of the Ephesians passage, of living and loving like Jesus, of rejoicing in our identity as beloved children, and of imitating God.

Imitating God

Recently, I was listening to the radio when a local Catholic priest was speaking about salvation. He argued salvation was through Jesus alone, was accomplished through his atoning sacrifice on the cross, and was available only through the One True Church—the Roman Catholic Church. Sadly, many Christians would be offended by only his last statement. We're comfortable with Christian exclusivity unless we're the ones left out.

For many, the central message of Christianity is that God's presence, affection, and interest is limited to a relative few. God loves some and rejects the rest. The reason for this rejection varies. For some, it's fate—some are chosen and some are not. For others, it's freedom—some choose to respond and be saved and others don't. Gracious Christianity, in contrast, rejects any understanding of God's love that isn't universal and eternal.

I believe we imitate God when we love all persons, convinced of their ultimate salvation. This is not a distinctively Christian belief, since people of many faiths share this confidence. But as Christians, we have the additional good fortune of having the words and example of Jesus. He offered his life not as a sacrifice to a bloodthirsty God, but as an example of faithful integrity. Unfortunately, his gracious invitation to the good life has often been presented as a divine demand.

"I am the way, and the truth, and the life. No one comes to the Father except through me" (John 14:6). There is no passage of Scripture I hear more often from those who oppose my beliefs than this one. They insist only those who accept Jesus as the divine Son of God, the Messiah and Savior of the World, can claim the title Christian. Though I suspect the writer of John's Gospel shared their opinion, even this passage is open to interpretation. What does it mean to come to the Father through Jesus?

According to John, Jesus went on to explain what he meant. Immediately after Jesus's bold statement, Philip, one of his disciples, asked, "Lord, show us the Father, and we will be satisfied." Apparently, he too found Jesus's words confusing.

Jesus answered, "Have I been with you all this time, Philip, and you still do not know me? Whoever has seen me has seen the Father. How can you say, 'Show us the Father'? Do you not believe I am in the Father and the Father is in me? The words that I say to you I do not speak on my own; but the Father who dwells in me does his works. Believe me that I am in the Father and the Father is in me; *but if you do not,* then believe me because of the works themselves" (John 14:8–11; italics added).

Jesus did not claim divinity in this passage, but the presence of God within him. He said his life and words reflected the values of God, that we could see God in him. Jesus was not primarily concerned with what we believed about him. He acknowledged that some wouldn't believe God was present in him. He hoped they would recognize God in his works—his way of life.

It is the way of Jesus, and not Jesus as the way, that is crucial. Traditional Christianity has largely ignored this distinction. In emphasizing Jesus as the one who saves the world, we've made his way of living insignificant, if not irrelevant.

One of my critics asked, "If everyone is going to be saved, why bother with Jesus?" In a moment of rare spontaneous inspiration, I answered, "I've never considered Jesus a bother."

I explained why I imitate Jesus—not because he is divine and the only way to God—but because I'm persuaded that when Christians live as graciously as Jesus, we imitate God and participate in God's work in the world. Jesus led his disciples in a revolutionary way of living with a new set of principles. If it hadn't been revolutionary, he wouldn't have been killed.

In the passage I cited above, Jesus went on to say, "They who have my commandments and keep them are those who love me" (John 14:21). It is not enough to believe in a particular identity of Jesus—Son of God, Messiah, Lord, Savior, and so forth. We cannot divorce belief from lifestyle. Dietrich Bonhoeffer wrote, "Only he who believes is obedient, and only he who is obedient believes."[2] But what do we obey? Does Christianity replace one rigid system of commands with another? Fortunately, the only commands Jesus seemed interested in were the commands to love.

When Jesus was asked what commands we must obey, he said, "You shall love the Lord your God with all your heart, and with all your soul, and with all your mind.... You shall love your neighbor as yourself" (Matthew 22:37–39). This second commandment is the core principle of gracious Christianity.

Gracious Christianity is committed to the principles of Jesus, of which loving our neighbor is primary. If there was any doubt about the primacy of this command to love God by loving our neighbor, Jesus dispelled it by concluding, "On these two commandments hang all the law and the prophets" (Matthew 22:40). When we fail to fulfill this command, we diminish his teaching. When we limit our understanding of neighbor to our church, denomination, nationality, or religious persuasion, we take Jesus's name in vain. When we lift up this commandment of Jesus—to love our neighbors—we draw all people to God and one another.

The chief difference between traditional Christianity and gracious Christianity is an insistence on seeing every person as our neighbor, now and forever. All are children of God and brothers and sisters, even those who consider themselves our enemies. Their disregard does not alter Jesus's command one iota.

Jesus clarified this in an additional commandment: "You have heard it was said, 'You should love your neighbor and hate your enemy.' But I say to you, Love your enemies and pray for those who persecute you, so that you may be children of your Father in heaven. . . . Be perfect, therefore, as your heavenly Father is perfect" (Matthew 5:43–44, 48). In loving our enemies, we are imitators of God. Perfection is not in keeping some religious code, but in being gracious to the ungracious.

But how do we accomplish this difficult task in our daily lives? Fortunately, Jesus offered a helpful guideline: "Do to others as you would have them do to you" (Luke 6:31). Jesus asks us to reflect on what we desire, then give the same to others. We are not to do to others what they've done to us, but to break the cycle of hate and hostility by doing the good.

In light of this principle alone, I relinquish the claim that all must approach God through Jesus. I wouldn't want Buddhists, Hindus, Muslims, or Jews to insist I approach God through their tradition or prophets. I refuse to threaten others with damnation and hell, because I don't respond well to such condemnation. I value gentleness, humility, openness, and compassion, because I appreciate when others are gentle, humble, open, and compassionate toward me.

I'm no longer interested in converting people of other faiths. Freed from the pressure of having to snatch them from the pit, I've committed to living my life in such a way that others are drawn to God. This is not a concept alien to Christianity. I was reminded when I was growing up that I might be the only Bible anyone ever read. This lifestyle evangelism reorders my priorities. I focus on being loving and gracious instead of converting and recruiting. Traditional Christian evangelism is often ungracious.

Seyyed Hossein Nasr, in his book *The Heart of Islam,* says, "Many Christian missionaries have tried and still try to propagate Christianity not through the teachings of Christ alone, but mostly by the appeal of material aid such as rice and medicine, given in the name of Christian charity, but with the goal of conversion."[3] He describes how offensive this is to most Muslims.

I was initially puzzled by how feeding and caring for others was offensive. Yet Nasr points out how insidious such charity can be. We give rice and medicine to those we think likely to become Christians. Our motive is not simply to care for hungry or ill persons. We take advantage of their physical vulnerability and suffering in order to convert them.

I'd like to ignore his critique, but I remember how early in my ministry, when people would come asking for food, I'd give away groceries with a generous serving of guilt. Why weren't they attending church? Why did they expect us to help them? Maybe if they started living more righteously, they wouldn't be in such a fix? Too often Christian charity comes with strings attached. We misunderstand our commission.

Jesus said, "Go therefore and make disciples of all nations, baptizing them in the name of the Father and of the Son and of the Holy Spirit, and teaching them to obey everything that I have commanded you. And remember, I am with you always, to the end of the age" (Matthew 28:19–20). Once again, I fear the Church has emphasized the wrong part of this passage. We've spent all our time and energy on making converts—baptizing others—and little effort in making disciples of Jesus—men and women committed to loving their neighbors and enemies, of doing to others what they desire for themselves, of being gracious in order to imitate God.

Gracious Christianity is committed to the lifestyle of Jesus, confident that living his way of life can usher in the kingdom of God. It trusts that God still moves and acts in the world, not simply in Christians, but in anyone who commits to loving neighbor and enemy. Convinced of the ultimate salvation of all people, it can focus on living in the present rather than worrying about the future. Gracious Christianity doesn't demand that people accept Jesus as Lord and Savior, but invites people to consider his example and to imitate his way.

A Gracious Lifestyle

At the turn of the twentieth century, long before Christians began to wear bracelets with the letters "WWJD," Charles Sheldon wrote a provocative novel entitled *In His Steps.* The premise of his book was that a group of Christians decided to ask the question, "What would Jesus do?" prior to making a decision or taking an action. Though the answers reflect the sensibilities of that time and the prejudices of the writer, the book suggested Jesus was far more than a sacrificial lamb. Sheldon thought Christians should imitate Jesus.

But which Jesus? The portrayal of Jesus in the Gospels is uneven, with variations in the story, with some incidents that seem more credible than others, and with the theological agendas of the authors influencing what Jesus says and does. Every attempt to reclaim the historical Jesus can be accused of manipulating Jesus. Mel Gibson's movie *The Passion of the Christ,* though it presented itself as a historic recreation, probably told us more about Mel Gibson than it did about Jesus. How do we escape the accusation, often valid, that Jesus ends up looking remarkably like us?

One solution is to acknowledge Jesus was like many of us. He struggled to know and understand God. He questioned and challenged many assumptions. He learned through trial and error. He developed, over time, a set of core principles that emphasized relationship over religious conformity. In so doing, Jesus becomes an example of the struggle and process rather than the answer to every question.

What would Jesus do in a given circumstance? I don't know, but he seemed to always seek the gracious way. This was no easier for him than it is for us. He wasn't always able to practice what he preached. The inconsistencies in Jesus's life aren't reason to ignore him, but encouragement for taking him seriously.

Having said that, I need to begin with a story I question. According to the Bible, there was one group of people with whom Jesus was not gracious. He ate with sinners, touched lepers, honored Romans, and recognized Samaritans, but Jesus is portrayed as being hateful toward Pharisees. Matthew 23 contains a long litany of accusations and denunciations in which Jesus repeatedly insults and curses this group of people.

Now it could be that Jesus did rail at the Pharisees. Even though he'd taught his disciples to love their enemies, he may have come to the end of his rope. I've not always responded graciously to my critics. On many occasions, I've said things that contradicted my theology and demonstrated how much more I have to learn about grace. Perhaps Jesus had a bad day.

But, far more likely, this passage of Scripture represents how quickly the Church abandoned the principles of Jesus and began to portray the Pharisees, who were the other major reformation movement within Judaism, as hypocrites. The Church made them enemies of Jesus and put its curses in Jesus's mouth. There is considerable historic and literary evidence of this pattern in the early Church, but even that isn't my primary reason for suspecting Jesus never attacked the Pharisees. I don't think Jesus acted this way toward his opponents because he taught me not to act that way toward mine.

Many times I've been tempted to apply the condemnations of Matthew 23 to my critics, to call them hypocrites, blind fools, and whitewashed tombs, to defend God's grace with words of wrath. It simply doesn't work. In so doing, I become the hypocrite. How we treat our critics is the clearest indication of our theology.

Fortunately, not all of Jesus's words for his opponents were caustic. He said: "Jerusalem, Jerusalem, the city that kills the prophets and stones those who are sent to it! How often have I desired to gather your children together as a hen gathers her brood under her wings, and you were not willing!" (Matthew 23:37). These are gentle, humble, open, and compassionate words. Let me share four stories that incarnate a gracious lifestyle of gentleness, humility, openness, and compassion.

One day, Jesus was resting by a well when a woman approached. That she was alone and drawing water in the middle of the day was telling. The other women of her village had apparently shunned her. When Jesus asked her for a drink, she asked, "How is it that you, a Jew, ask a drink of me, a woman of Samaria?" (John 4:9). She was surprised Jesus even acknowledged her.

Jesus accepted her as she was. He didn't treat her with the hostility she expected. He listened to her story—a long litany of failed relationships. Rather than condemning her, he spoke of the meaning of life and of God without using complicated theological language or arguments, without judging her behavior or her beliefs. Rather than demanding she adopt orthodox Judaism, he said, "God is spirit, and those who worship him must worship in spirit and truth" (John 4:24). Jesus was gentle, reading between the lines and responding to her need. Imitating him, gracious Christianity listens to where people are instead of telling them where they should be.

I learned this lesson from one of my most ardent opponents. I mentioned earlier in the book that one of my critics wrote a letter suggesting I be horsewhipped, though he later apologized. Let me tell you about his apology.

One Sunday morning, he showed up at my church with a bag of rocks. That Sunday I happened to be out of town. It's probably just as well. If I'd seen him carrying those rocks in the front, I'd have been sneaking out the back. My congregation, who knew of his animosity, was nervous when, at the end of the service, he rose and walked to the front of the meeting room. A couple of people ducked out, fearing the worst. Instead, this man laid his rocks on the altar and said, "Forgive me. I won't be throwing rocks at your pastor anymore."

Though he and I still don't agree on many things, we agree Jesus has commanded us to love one another. Though he remains unconvinced of the power of grace to save all, he demonstrated how grace had changed him. His grace also changed me, for what he didn't know is that I'd been throwing rocks as well. When he dropped his, I was able to drop mine. His gentleness, where there should have been hostility, allowed us to hear one another again.

Jesus was gentle because God is gentle. God knows our deepest pains, hidden fears, checkered pasts, and personal prejudices. God is not a blacksmith, hammering us into rigid conformity, but a potter, shaping us carefully into something beautiful and useful. God comes gently, seeking to be in relationship with us, but never violating our integrity. God, the creator of the universe, also comes humbly. Jesus demonstrated this humility.

One evening, before the evening meal, Jesus took a basin, took off his outer clothes, and wrapped a towel around his waist. Then he washed the feet of each of his disciples. This was not simply a symbolic gesture. In his day, people wearing sandals and walking dusty roads could expect their host or their host's servant to wash their feet. Some scholars speculate the disciples took turns performing this chore. Whatever the case, on this night the task fell to Jesus.

When he had finished, he said, "Do you know what I've done to you? You call me Teacher and Lord—and you are right, for that is what I am. So if I, your Lord and Teacher, have washed your feet, you also ought to wash one another's feet. For I have set you an example, that you also should do as I have done to you" (John 13:12–15). I wonder what the Church would be like if we had committed ourselves to washing one another's feet every Sunday instead of taking Communion? Jesus was humble, willing to take the servant's role. Imitating Jesus, gracious Christianity is more committed to relationship and reconciliation than position and power.

My father tells the story of an especially acrimonious church meeting in which two men, both good men and respected leaders, found themselves passionately advocating opposing viewpoints. In the heat of the discussion, both men became ungracious toward one another. Matt, one of the men, suddenly rose and stormed out of the meeting. Everyone was shocked, since this kind of behavior was out of character.

Fifteen minutes later, Matt returned with a basin of water in his hands, a towel over his shoulder, and tears in his eyes. He knelt before his opponent, removed his shoes and socks, and began to wash his feet. When he'd finished, he said, "Please forgive me. I've treated you very poorly. I realized after I left that, if you were so passionate about this issue, there must be a good reason. I need to listen to you because, even if we disagree, your opinion is important to me."

God thinks our opinion is important. I love the story in Exodus in which, after the people of Israel have built a golden calf, God considers destroying them and starting over. Moses defends the people and says, "Turn from your fierce wrath; change your mind and do not bring disaster on your people" (Exodus 32:12). God changes his mind. This is a humble God, open to critique and input.

One day, Jesus was traveling through a Gentile region when a woman began to beg him to heal her daughter. Jesus told her, "I was sent only to the lost sheep of the house of Israel. . . . It is not fair to take the children's food and throw it to the dogs." The woman said, "Yes, Lord, yet even the dogs eat the crumbs that fall from their masters' table" (Matthew 15:24–27).

I was taught, since Jesus was perfect, that his response couldn't be as racist and exclusive as it seems. I was told Jesus was testing the woman, to see how much faith she had, knowing full well he would heal the child in the end. I no longer make excuses for Jesus. I allow him to learn, to grow, to be transformed by the persistence of a woman who wouldn't accept an understanding of God that excluded her. Jesus was open, willing to allow others to challenge his thoughts and behaviors, allowing God to speak to him through those he might ignore. Imitating him, gracious Christians believe everyone we meet has something to teach us.

Ten years ago, Ronnie invited me to the worship service at the county jail. Ronnie had spent a couple of years in jail after nearly killing a man in a bar fight. He'd been saved while in jail, but when he grew angry the blood vessel in his temple would still throb and he'd clench his fists.

Actually, Ronnie had invited me four or five times. Each time I couldn't go, that blood vessel throbbed a little harder and his fists clenched a little tighter. He must have sensed what was true—I didn't want to go. I even began to schedule other events and appointments on the nights of the jail services so I would have an excuse.

One Sunday, after I'd preached a sermon on Matthew 25, Ronnie asked me why I didn't care about Jesus. Those were shocking words for a preacher to hear, but he pointed out that Jesus said, "I was in prison and you visited me" (Matthew 25:36). He asked, "You ever visit Jesus in prison, preacher?" He wasn't smiling. So I gave in. I thought, "I'll go once, tell him it isn't my calling, and that'll be the end of it." I've been spending time in prisons and jails ever since. Indeed, some of my most powerful experiences of grace have occurred behind prison bars. Jesus calls us to grow in every situation, to learn compassion for all.

One day, a rich young man approached Jesus and asked, "What must I do to inherit eternal life?" Jesus suggested the young man keep the commandments: not to commit murder or adultery, not to steal or lie, and to honor his parents. The young man said, "Teacher, I have kept all these since my youth." Then Mark adds a verse sadly absent from the other Gospels. Mark writes, "Jesus, looking at him, loved him." Though Jesus challenged the young man to live more graciously, to rid himself of his wealth, and to care for the poor, Jesus clearly saw in the young man a desire to please God. When he "went away grieving, for he had many possessions" (Mark 10:17–22), Jesus suffered with him. Jesus was compassionate, understanding how difficult it is for us to leave any treasured possession behind, be it material or theological. Imitating him, gracious Christians look with love on those unwilling or unable to step forward in gracious faith.

I realize that what I am asking of traditional Christianity is difficult. For so long, we've held the keys to the kingdom. We've thought ourselves in sole possession of the truth. We've carefully guarded the gates of heaven. We've been unwilling to sacrifice power, prestige, and pride in order to care for the poor of the world. In the process, I fear we've become old wineskins. Jesus said, "No one puts new wine into old wineskins; otherwise, the wine will burst the skins, and the wine is lost, and so are the skins; but one puts new wine into fresh wineskins" (Mark 2:22). In order for grace to flourish, we will need to reform more than our theology. We will need to remake the Church.

A Gracious Church

A couple of years ago, a Quaker meeting in our area performed a same-sex marriage. This was not well received in other Quaker meetings. One meeting wrote a scathing letter condemning the marriage and homosexuality. Its members made it clear homosexuals were not welcome in their meeting. A few days later, I happened to drive by their meetinghouse. On the sign outside, in large letters, were the words, "Everyone welcome."

The first and most important change in the Church is to truly open our doors to all people. If everyone will someday stand hand in hand before God, we need to invite them to stand with us now. A lack of hospitality, the willingness to warmly welcome whoever comes, has been a blight on the Church. Even when the Church has allowed the "unacceptable" inside its doors, we've often greeted them coldly and seated them in the balcony.

As a young man, I had a beard and long hair. Ironically, I looked a lot like the picture of Jesus hanging in our church. People tolerated my appearance, but made certain I knew of their disapproval. I remember how painful it was for me to withstand this censure. I can only imagine how difficult it is for the more despised to enter the doors of the Church.

Mere tolerance is not enough. A Church that claims to be the Body of Christ must act like Jesus. We must reach out and touch the lepers, call them brothers and sisters, and seek their healing and restoration to the community. This must happen before they repent of whatever we deem sinful, and not afterward. They must be accepted as they are. In the process, change will come. Either they will find the courage to become different, or we will discover our judgments were wrong.

The doors of the Church have been guarded for too long. Again and again, the Church has identified who is welcome and who is not. Dualism has encouraged this un-graciousness, but even if we believe God will welcome some to heaven and reject others, we have no excuse for excluding some here on earth. Jesus said, "Do not judge, so that you may not be judged. For with the judgment you make you will be judged, and the measure you give will be the measure you get" (Matthew 7:1–2). Too often, the Church acts as judge, jury, and executioner.

Unfortunately, though we often look back with shame on our mistakes, we don't seem to learn from them. What pains me is that so soon after the Church's repentance for its support of segregation and racism we've begun justifying and rationalizing the rejection of another group of people—homosexuals.

It is crucial to understand that welcoming homosexuals into the Church is not a moral issue. It really doesn't matter whether we agree with their lifestyle or not. We are called to love them, not judge them. We are called to be gracious. If we fail to be gracious, we fail to obey a command far more central to Christianity than sexual orientation. We forget that every person the Church welcomes is morally flawed. No one will arrive in heaven perfected—we will all need transformation. The Church, offering a foretaste of heaven, should be a place where people come to be accepted, loved, healed, and restored.

Philip Yancey tells a story of a prostitute who, homeless, sick, and unable to feed her two-year-old, rented her daughter out for kinky sex. The person counseling her asked if she had ever thought of going to church. "Church!" she cried. "Why would I ever go there? I was already feeling terrible about myself. They'd just make me feel worse."[4]

That prostitute knew what the Psalmist lamented—our sins are ever before us (Psalm 51:3). She didn't need salt in her wounds. She needed healing. People may, for a time, ignore the misery, pain, grief, and harm they cause themselves and others, but it's a sham. Eventually, they will turn and seek help. I've never found it necessary to stand on street corners reminding people of their need for transformation. People knock on the church door and, in a hundred different ways, say, "Save me!"

They are not asking us to point out their sinfulness, to invite them to the altar, or to lead them in the prayer of salvation. They are asking us to demonstrate another way of life—an alternative to whatever destructive path they've been on. It isn't, as I've been accused of, a matter of ignoring their sin, but in celebrating their worth. This is what Jesus modeled when he refused to sanction the stoning of the woman caught in adultery. He told her to "sin no more" only after he'd convinced her of his love (John 8:3–11).

Often people joke, when I invite them to church, that the ceiling might fall in. I wish they simply misunderstood the character of the Church, but I suspect they reflect the image we've created. We've portrayed the Church as a social club rather than a hospital. The truth is that the Church is a gathering of wounded and broken people relying on the grace of God as they struggle to heal and grow. Henri Nouwen explains this dynamic with a rabbinic story:

Rabbi Yoshua ben Levi asked Elijah, "When will the Messiah come?"

"Go and ask him yourself."

"Where is he?"

"Sitting at the gates of the city."

"How shall I know him?"

"He is sitting among the poor covered with wounds. The others unbind all their wounds at the same time and then bind them up again. But he unbinds one at a time and binds it up again, saying, 'Perhaps I shall be needed: if so I must always be ready so as not to delay for a moment.'"[5]

Jesus said, "Those who are well have no need of a physician, but those who are sick. Go and learn what this means,

'I desire mercy, not sacrifice.' For I have come to call not the righteous but sinners" (Matthew 9:12–13). Jesus calls the wounded to follow. When we think ourselves spiritually superior, there is no need to follow Jesus. When we acknowledge our brokenness, we are free to heal and be healed.

Everyone is welcome because everyone is wounded and broken, from the back pew to the pulpit. As a pastor, I've learned to step off the pedestal and reveal my struggles, doubts, and failures. When I'm honest, others become more vulnerable. The week after I admitted to a battle with pornography, three men called and asked for help with their own addictions. Unfortunately, the Church has often asked pastors and leaders to be inauthentic.

Patrick Means, in his book *Men's Secret Wars,* reports on a survey of Church leaders. Sixty-four percent acknowledged struggling with some sexual addiction or compulsion. Twenty-five percent admitted to sexual indiscretions outside of marriage.[6] Means discovered Church leaders had the same rates of sexual dysfunction as the general population. However, within traditional Christianity, where grace is measured in teaspoons, pastors know better than to admit their struggles and sins. We want symbols of perfection rather than leaders with clay feet. Many pastors would gladly give up this pretense. Those who covet it are dangerous.

Traditional Christianity has been authoritarian. Pastors rule small kingdoms in which their word is law. Clergy are honored and laity are ignored. George Fox, the founder of Quakerism, found this so objectionable he accused the clergy of being "hirelings"—motivated by money and power rather than grace. When I became a Quaker pastor, this critique bothered me. Ellen, one of the members of my congregation, put me at ease. She said, "Don't worry. We'll remind you as often as possible that you are just one of us."

A gracious Church is one that avoids distinctions conferring special status, prestige, or authority. Bishops, priests, and pastors are not called to greater power, but to more intentional and specific service. They are not immune to error or bestowed with special gifts. Whatever authority they have should be in response to what others experience in them.

Dom Helder Camara is one such example. Camara, twice nominated for the Nobel Peace Prize, served as "the bishop to the poor" in Brazil. Not only did he challenge inappropriate political power, he asked many probing questions of the Church. At the closing session of Vatican II, he suggested all the cardinals and bishops lay their gold and silver crosses at the feet of the pope, to be melted down and used to serve the poor.

Camara was a critic of clerical privilege and authority. He said, "If there is a crisis of authority, it may also be because we who are in authority forget that exercising authority means serving, not being served. Authoritarian authority is impossible nowadays: authority can stem only from dialogue and mutual, fraternal consideration."[7] This distinction, being authoritarian versus being authoritative, is crucial to a gracious Church. A Church in which leaders dictate is a dictatorship.

In a gracious Church, men and women become authoritative. Their lives attract others and give weight to their words and thoughts. Quakers call these men and women "weighty Friends." These people, by virtue of their lives, have earned the right to be heard. They also tend to be people who seldom speak. They listen long and hard and share their insights only after careful reflection.

Although authority is earned, membership should be freely given. There is probably no more ungracious practice within the Church than membership. It is the way we control, manipulate, influence, and separate. It is not a reflection of commitment and spiritual maturity, but a sign of status. Fifty percent of all Church members do not even attend worship regularly. The answer isn't to trim our rolls; it is to redefine membership.

Membership in the Church doesn't begin when someone goes through Confirmation, gets baptized, or makes some wooden confession of faith. Membership in the Church happens whenever we act like Jesus. If the Church is the Body of Christ, whenever the needs of the world are being met, the Church is present. Belonging to a religious institution is not belonging to the Church.

Once again, I suspect dualism has much to do with our obsession with membership. We like to count heads. Who is in and who is out? Who is saved and who is lost? In belonging to a religious institution, we imply there is an identity more important than belonging to the human race and being a child of God. Belonging to the Church is not a status. It is a responsibility. Those who know the grace of God first have the responsibility to reach out to those who know it last.

When the distinctions between clergy and laity, member and nonmember disappear, we are not left with chaos. We are left with a Church in which all men and women are expected to take their spiritual journey seriously, where each person's contribution is valued and where there is space for all to learn and grow. A gracious Church is a safe place to ask questions, explore new ideas, admit our struggles, and seek assistance.

Sadly, this is not the nature of most congregations. Too often, a church is where people who already agree gather to have their viewpoints reinforced. When I first began preaching on universal salvation, Larry, a member of my congregation, told me an odd story. His friend had heard of my theology and had chastised Larry for believing in the salvation of all. Larry explained that he didn't believe in the salvation of all, but appreciated my point of view. His friend, even more disturbed, asked, "How can you attend a church where you don't believe everything the pastor believes?"

A better question is whether people should attend a church where they are expected to believe everything the pastor believes. Early in the history of the Church, many argued for precisely this conformity. Irenaeus, one of the early champions of orthodoxy, was suspicious of diversity. He accused all who disagreed with him of being heretics, frauds, and liars. He suggested Christians need not ask any further questions—all the important issues were resolved. Elaine Pagels notes, "He writes his massive, five-volume attack, *The Refutation and Overthrow of Falsely So-Called Knowledge,* to demand that members of his congregation stop listening to any of them [those who didn't agree with Irenaeus] and return to the basic foundation of their faith. Irenaeus promises that he will explain for them what the Scriptures really mean and insists that only what he teaches is true."[8] Unfortunately, his view of the Church won the day. Many pastors today act more like Irenaeus than Jesus.

We forget Jesus was accused of being a fraud and liar. The religious authorities of his time considered him unorthodox and dangerous. He asked and encouraged questions. He told stories that required reflection. He challenged the assumptions of his day. He commanded his disciples to love God with heart, soul, strength, and mind. He told his disciples to ask, seek, and knock. He wasn't threatened by doubt.

A gracious Church is a place where people can come with questions, doubts, and struggles without fear of being condemned. Our focus is not on supplying quick and easy answers to difficult problems, but creating the space to think and explore. In the midst of our theological struggle, a gracious Church reminds us of what really matters—how we treat those around us.

The final characteristic of a gracious Church is compassion. To be compassionate is to suffer with the world. Traditional Christianity emphasizes Jesus's suffering for the world. Rather than seeing the cross as a symbol of Christian commitment, it becomes a symbol of one man's sacrifice. Yet even Jesus didn't understand the cross this way. He said, "If any want to become my followers, let them deny themselves and take up their cross daily and follow me" (Luke 9:23).

The cross is a symbol of Jesus's willingness to absorb pain, to share the most brutal of human conditions, and to demonstrate grace and forgiveness to the bitter end. The authenticity of Jesus's commands to love our neighbors and enemies is confirmed by his willingness to forgive both Jew and Roman from the cross. A gracious Church is a Church willing to pull the cross down from its steeple and shoulder it in the world.

Clarence Jordan tells of a pastor giving him a tour of a multimillion-dollar church facility: "It was one of those graceful swooping things that went up into a big, beautiful cross way up on top and he pointed to it and he said, 'Even our cross cost us $10,000.' And I said, 'Brother, you got gypped. The time was you could get them for nothing.'"[9]

That's still true. You can still get a cross for free. When I think of the way of the cross, I think of Father Damien. He was a Belgian priest who, in 1863, was sent by the Catholic Church to Hawaii. He went there unaware that Hawaii was in the throes of a terrible leprosy epidemic. Hundreds were catching this disfiguring and fatal disease. And this was in a day when leprosy was still thought to be caused by sexual immorality. Lepers were seen by many as both physical and spiritual outcasts.

Father Damien arrived in Hawaii as officials there began to collect the lepers and exile them to the island of Molokai. Stranded there with only the barest essentials and no medical care, many quickly died. Father Damien protested and in 1873 was allowed to establish Kalapapa, a colony for lepers. He built a church, hospital, homes, and school. He recruited doctors and nurses. He pestered the Church and the government to provide funds. He sought research into the causes of the disease and argued it wasn't caused by sexual immorality. Most of all, Father Damien refused to be afraid of his parish of lepers. He touched and hugged them even though he knew the risk.

In 1883, he began to feel a tingling in his own leg—he too had contracted leprosy. His superiors in the Church and government accused him of sexual immorality, but allowed him to remain at Kalapapa, since no parish would have accepted a priest with leprosy. For the next six years, he labored to build the colony into a place of comfort and compassion. But on April 2, 1889, he finally died of complications from his disease.

In 1959, when Hawaii became a state, it was allowed to place two statues of state heroes in the Capitol. One was of Father Damien. The world recognizes acts of grace. It also knows how often the Church has been ungracious. Christianity will earn the right to speak to the world when we finally live and act like Jesus. Then, and only then, will we be able to transform the kingdoms of this world into the kingdom of God.

1. Elaine Pagels, *Beyond Belief: The Secret Gospel of Thomas* (New York: Random House, 2003), p. 37. Pagels, the premier scholar on the Gnostic gospels, offers powerful insight into the diversity of the early Church.
2. Dietrich Bonhoeffer, *The Cost of Discipleship* (New York: Macmillan, 1949), p. 69. This book challenges us to understand the interplay between grace and discipleship.
3. Seyyed Hossein Nasr, *The Heart of Islam* (San Francisco: HarperSan-Francisco, 2002), p. 47. This is a helpful survey of Islam and a pointed critique of Christian arrogance.
4. Philip Yancey, *What's So Amazing About Grace?* (Grand Rapids, MI: Zondervan, 1997), p. 11. Yancey offers one of the most beautiful descriptions of grace from a traditional Christian perspective. His is as gracious as such theology can be.
5. Henri Nouwen, *The Wounded Healer* (Garden City, NY: Doubleday, 1972), p. 82. Nouwen models humble Christian leadership.
6. Patrick Means, *Men's Secret Wars* (Grand Rapids, MI: Revell, 1996), p. 132. This book is a terrific tool for diagnosing and addressing the guilt and shame traditional Christianity often heaps on men.
7. Dom Helder Camara, *The Conversations of a Bishop* (New York: Collins, 1977), p. 170. Camara is one of the lesser-known saints of the twentieth century.
8. Pagels, *Beyond Belief,* p. 142.
9. Clarence Jordan, *The Substance of Faith* (New York: Association, 1972), p. 109. This crusty Southern Baptist preacher wasn't always gracious, but he was prophetic.

7

The Politics of Grace

In 1980, in response to the Soviet Union's invasion of Afghanistan, President Jimmy Carter reinstated the Selective Service program requiring young men to register. Those who didn't could no longer receive federal funds for college. Since I was preparing to attend college, I faced a dilemma. A pacifist, I was opposed to war and its preparation, but I had also counted on those grants and loans. After much soul searching, I decided not to register at the local post office.

One of my friends marched down to the post office on his eighteenth birthday to register. Later that day, he asked me if I'd registered. I said I hadn't and didn't plan to.

He was scandalized. He spoke of his love of country, his responsibility as a citizen, and finally his obedience as a Christian. He reminded me that the Bible says, "Render therefore unto Caesar the things which be Caesar's." He failed to quote the remainder of the verse, "and unto God the things which be God's" (Luke 20:25, KJV). Certain he'd made an ironclad case, he asked how I, a fellow Christian, could refuse to register.

I spoke of Jesus' command not to kill, to turn the other cheek, and to love the enemy. I reminded him of Peter's statement to the Sanhedrin when they ordered him to stop preaching about Jesus: "We must obey God rather than any human authority" (Acts 5:29). He insisted that verse wasn't in the Bible and was shocked when, even in the King James Version, he found such words.

We were young, arrogant, and convinced of our righteousness. We each thought ourselves morally superior to the other. We were both willing to sacrifice for what we believed. Neither of us really listened to the other. Our conversation mirrored a tension that still exists among religious people of all stripes—how to be citizens in this world while valuing our commitment to the principles of God. Or, stated differently, how do we mix religion and politics?

In the churches of my youth, religion and politics were separated by a wide moat. We were encouraged to be law-abiding citizens, to vote, and to be patriotic, but we were also reminded Christ's kingdom was not of this world. We sang, "This world is not my home. I'm just a-passing through." Politics was thought to be a worldly business, full of deceit, hardly the proper sphere for a good Christian.

In this theology, worldliness was evil. We were strangers and aliens in this world. We were to be in the world, but not of the world. The Bible, we were taught, forbid any alliance with the world. "Adulterers! Do you not know that friendship with the world is enmity with God? Therefore whoever wishes to be a friend of the world becomes an enemy of God" (James 4:4). Being a politician was spiritual adultery.

Adding to our aversion was our confidence that the kingdoms of this world were doomed. We believed in Christ's imminent return. Not only was the world evil; it was a waste of time to try to improve it. Liberal churches, with their social programs and political activism, were mocked. Why should we strive for peace, justice, and goodness in a world soon to be ruled by the Antichrist and destined for destruction? Faithful Christians labored for souls, while liberal Christians dabbled in politics, to no good end.

In college, I became uncomfortable with this division between the spiritual and the worldly. More accurately, Tony Campolo made me uncomfortable. In a chapel service at our conservative Christian college, Campolo began his remarks with these words, "According to United Nation's statistics, approximately ten thousand people starved to death last night, and most of you don't give a shit."

Our gasp was audible.

He continued, "The problem is that most of you are more upset I used the word 'shit' than you are over the fact that ten thousand people starved to death last night."

In his book *The Challenge of Social Action,* Campolo writes, "The kingdom which Jesus initiated is a new social order composed of people who are obedient to the will of

God, who structure their lives and their social institutions in accord with His desires and maintain a system of human relationships that reflect His love and justice. Jesus wants to create a revolutionary new society."[1]

After hearing Tony Campolo speak, I was convinced Christians could and should change the world. I was not alone. In the 1970s, millions of Christians became politically active. With the *Roe* v. *Wade* decision legalizing abortion, conservative Christians began to mobilize. Jerry Falwell marshaled the forces of the Moral Majority. Pat Robertson recruited troops through his television network. Ralph Reed, president of the Christian Coalition, bragged of systematically taking control of the political machinery of the Republican Party. Across the country, conservative churches distributed score cards rating politicians on their allegiance to "Christian" values. Conservatives bridged the moat and stormed the castle.

I applauded this activism then and I applaud it now. Though I've come to disagree with much of the agenda of conservative Christianity, I believe Christians (as well as Muslims, Buddhists, Hindus, Jews, and others) should be represented at the political table. As a Christian, I'm responsible to the principles of Jesus—to love neighbor and enemy, to seek justice and equality, to live graciously in an ungracious world. Since Jesus was living in the shadow of a brutal imperial dictatorship, it's hard to say precisely what he would have suggested to those living in a democratic society, but it wouldn't have been passivity or apathy.

Jesus, though never commanding his disciples to be politically active, did tell them to be a city on a hill, a light, salt,
and leaven. Though never advocating a violent revolution,
Jesus said the poor, the diseased, and the downtrodden
would inherit the earth and be called the children of God.
The kingdom of God was within them. Their poverty and
powerlessness wasn't an excuse for inactivity. His followers
were to transform the world.

Though many of Jesus's followers came from the bottom
of the heap, Jesus had a vision for those on the top as well.
He warned them that the first would be last and the exalted
would be humbled. He challenged the wealthy and powerful
to work toward economic equality. The rich and powerful
had a responsibility to care for "the least." Whether for the
rich or the poor, Jesus's words were not politically neutral.

John Howard Yoder, a little-known yet exceptional
theologian and scholar, writes:

> Jesus was not just a moralist whose teachings had
> some political implications; he was not primarily a
> teacher of spirituality whose public ministry unfor-
> tunately was seen in a political light; he was not just
> a sacrificial lamb preparing for his immolation, or a
> God-Man whose divine status calls us to disregard
> his humanity. Jesus was, in his divinely mandated
> prophethood, priesthood, and kingship, the bearer of
> a new possibility of human, social, and therefore po-
> litical relationships. His baptism is the inauguration

and his cross is the culmination of that new regime in which his disciples are called to share.[2]

The question is not whether we should mix Christianity and politics. To follow Jesus is to be political. The issue is whether our understanding of Christianity makes the world more gracious or less gracious. Do we work against injustice, oppression, greed, and self-absorption, or do we defend the status quo? Do we take seriously Jesus's call to "bring good news to the poor, . . . proclaim release to the captives and . . . let the oppressed go free" (Luke 4:18), or do we treat Jesus as our team mascot? Republicans and Democrats, liberals and conservatives all face these temptations.

This was why the churches of my childhood were so suspicious of politics. Ralph Reed, in his book *Active Faith: How Christians Are Changing the Soul of American Politics,* admits that, though Christians have every right and reason to be politically active, they must be careful. He warns: "As a community of faith, we stand at a crossroads. Down one path lies the fate of many other great religiously inspired political movements of the past: irrelevance and obscurity. It is a path defined by its spiritual arrogance and by its faulty assumption that the most efficacious way to change the hearts of men and women is through the coercive power of the state. . . . It is not the right path for our movement."[3] Coercion is never the right path.

Politics, though informed by and sensitive to religious ethics, should never become the handmaiden of any one re-

ligion or sect. If history is any indication, when dogmatic religion and unprincipled politics merge, grace dies. When
ideologies clash, there can be only one victor, and the political landscape will be littered with the casualties of war—
compromise, consensus, and community. When politics
becomes ungracious, no matter how noble and righteous the
cause, the priorities of God invariably suffer.

Ungracious Politics

My church, a mix of Democrats, Republicans, and Independents, enjoys a good-natured banter about politics. One recent Christmas, the Republicans gave me, their liberal minister, a nativity set. When I opened it, the man presenting it asked if I'd noticed what was missing. Sensing my confusion, he pointed out the set had no donkey. He announced, "This is a Republican nativity set."

Though I've never claimed to be a Democrat, I'll admit to finding liberal solutions to many social problems attractive. Unfortunately, I haven't found the Democratic Party or its politicians to be any more gracious than Republicans. I've found it increasingly difficult to get excited about any political party. Politics today is often hostile, full of innuendo, accusation, and personal attack.

I experienced this ugliness when I attended a rally in downtown Indianapolis to demonstrate my disapproval of our government's decision to go to war against Iraq in 2003. I wanted our nation to work with the United Nations in developing a plan that would police rather than destroy Iraq. I feared war would only create more terrorists. I am convinced violence always begets violence. Unfortunately, what I experienced at that peace rally was what I opposed—violence.

Speaker after speaker personally attacked the president, the vice president, and others in the administration. They accused the president of being a liar, of going to war in order to control Iraqi oil, of using the September 11 attack for political gain, and of generally being an evil person. Those who supported war were ridiculed. I finally left. I couldn't reconcile the violence of their rhetoric with my commitment to grace and peace.

I think President George W. Bush made mistakes in his handling of terrorism and the Iraqi situation, but I don't believe he is an evil person. He seemed sincere in his attempts to answer difficult societal issues, even though I disagree with many of his solutions. Though he is as susceptible to impure motives as anyone, I don't believe he sent thousands of soldiers to Iraq in order to increase the value of his stock portfolio. Gracious politics, at the very minimum, requires giving those with differing viewpoints the benefit of the doubt. They too are working for a better world.

Ungracious politics demonizes our opponents. Refusing to weigh their concerns and consider their point of view, we slander their motives and question their integrity. We create an atmosphere of distrust and hate. Whenever we attack individuals, rather than critique their ideas, we violate the principles of Jesus and perpetuate the battleground of politics.

Unfortunately, traditional Christianity has often given tacit support to this view of politics. Dualism, with its division between the righteous and the unrighteous, offers a pattern too easily transferred to politics. My party is righteous, and the other party is wicked. Only my party has the truth. Only my party can lead the way. Only my party loves our country. Only my party honors God. When our political platform is presented as a divine mandate, all those who offer other solutions are greedy and selfish or the pawns of Satan.

It is easy for us to recognize this distortion in other countries. When the Ayatollah Khomeini in Iran calls the United States "the great Satan," we roll our eyes. When the Taliban tears down ancient Buddha statues and beats women publicly for exposing their skin, we applaud its defeat. What we fail to see is how easily American politics can fall into this same trap. Unfortunately, in recent years, there have been indications we stand perilously close to this abyss.

Many Christians are unaware of a strong undercurrent in conservative Christianity promoting an American jihad. This movement, often referred to as reconstructionism or dominion theology, argues the United States is a Christian nation with the need to purify itself and dominate the world. Originating with a theologian named Rousas John Rushdoony, this movement works to reconstruct a rigid and harsh religious culture based on "biblical" principles. Once the United States is purified, it hopes to use military power to conquer the world. Frederick Clarkson, in *The Public Eye,* writes:

> Reconstructionism seeks to replace democracy with
> a theocratic elite that would govern by imposing

their interpretation of "Biblical Law." Reconstructionism would eliminate not only democracy but
many of its manifestations, such as labor unions,
civil rights laws, and public schools. Women would
be generally relegated to hearth and home. Insuffi-
ciently Christian men would be denied citizenship,
perhaps executed. So severe is this theocracy that
it would extend capital punishment beyond such
crimes as kidnapping, rape, and murder to include,
among other things, blasphemy, heresy, adultery,
and homosexuality.[4]

Gary Bauer, the president of the Family Research
Council, a domestic policy adviser to President Ronald Reagan, and a recent presidential candidate, represents the most
public manifestation of this theology. He argues we are in
the midst of a cultural war, with the winner getting the
right to teach the children. His vision of what the children
need to be taught is decidedly sectarian. Although his lack
of success as a presidential candidate may be comforting,
many within conservative Christian circles have adopted aspects of this theology.

When President Reagan spoke of the Soviet Union as
an "evil empire," he was expressing this theology. When
James Dobson of Focus on the Family accused homosexuals
of a conspiracy to attack the family, he was reflecting this
mind-set. When many conservative Christians speak of a
culture war, they aren't speaking metaphorically. Islamic

fundamentalism is not the only threat to freedom and democracy. Christian theologies that seek political means to enforce one perspective are equally dangerous.

Theocracy, the rule of God, is not the ideal. Human institutions, by their very nature, are flawed. No human government can claim divine ordination or perfection. Democracy, where every voice and perspective is valued, is the least dangerous political system. Within such a system, religious voices must be heard, but each as only one voice amid a large and varied choir. We are called to transform politics, not simply use it to achieve an agenda. Ungracious politics, even when waving a flag or a cross, violates the principles of Jesus.

Gracious politics will be gentle, humble, open, and compassionate. Through such politics we will love neighbor and enemy and treat others as we want to be treated. How to obey these principles in the political realm is open to debate; the need to respond is not. Christians should have an opinion on capital punishment, abortion, welfare, and homosexual unions. That sincere Christians will have differing opinions should highlight our need for gentleness and humility. More important, we must be open to the viewpoints of other religious traditions and philosophies. We must value and guard the public square. Together, with all people of conviction, we must move beyond self-interest and seek the common good.

Principled Politics

I miss Paul Simon. This senator from Illinois wasn't much to look at—short, plain, and forever attired in a bow tie—but there have been few politicians who match his compassion, integrity, and humility. He was a champion for the neglected. In Illinois, he spearheaded state legislation providing public education to children with disabilities and eventually sponsored this reform at the federal level. He worked tirelessly to see the Smithsonian open a museum honoring African American life and contributions. He consistently supported U.S. aid to impoverished countries.

He was honest and humble. In the 1950s, long before politicians were required to divulge their finances, he opened his books. He was an unflagging advocate of ethical reform, opposing the power of special-interest groups and criticizing people within his own party. He was vocal about President Clinton's ethical failures. Yet he admitted his own frailty. He was known to acknowledge his mistakes publicly and to admit when he'd voted incorrectly. This openness earned him the respect of senators on both sides of the aisle. In the hardball world of national politics, this is a rare feat.

He was a man of principles in a profession in which power and prestige rule. What many don't know, because he never flaunted his faith, was that Paul Simon was a passionate Christian. He sought to live his life in accordance with the principles of Jesus. His ability to practice the politics of grace without fanfare and in an age when televised political debate encourages the opposite marked him as a hero of grace for our times.

I'm suspicious when politicians speak too boldly and often of their religious convictions. For many politicians, "God-talk" is nothing more than window dressing, savvy public relations. Today, nearly every candidate claims membership in a church or synagogue. But what matters is not how vocal they are, but how gracious. Do they allow the priorities of a gracious God to inform their public life? This is the question whether you are a senator or a private citizen.

Loving your neighbor is a political command. We are our brother's keeper. We have a responsibility to feed the hungry, give drink to the thirsty, clothe the naked, shelter the homeless, heal the sick, and visit the imprisoned. When Jesus expanded the meaning of neighbor to include everyone, these Christian imperatives became political concerns. Being a good neighbor is more complicated than taking a pie across the street. Loving your neighbor means working for a just and equitable society in which every person is valued and respected. Though this commitment must begin in our neighborhood, city, state, and country, our concern must encompass the world.

How we accomplish this is complicated, and there will be many answers. Having worked in the inner city, I know the need for social programs such as welfare, food stamps, AFDC (Aid to Families with Dependent Children), WIC (Women and Infant Care), and the like. I also know how often these programs are abused and how easy it is for people to become institutionalized. Looking around the world, I recognize the need to address the AIDS epidemic, poverty, malnutrition, and the like. I also recognize these are complicated issues that don't always lend themselves to easy solutions.

The Republican emphasis on accountability and the Democratic emphasis on assistance are both legitimate. However, when politics is a battle, one emphasis must defeat the other rather than discover ways to incorporate both concerns. Gracious politics acknowledges we are all part of the community. Decision making becomes a matter of consensus, an effort to weave together the finer qualities of each perspective, rather than a throat grabbing quest for power.

My belief in the salvation of every person requires I value the worth and dignity of every person. An opposing viewpoint must be heard, even if that viewpoint is ultimately rejected. Others' concerns must be acknowledged. At the same time, whatever hampers a person's ability and opportunity to respond to God and be transformed must be challenged and resisted. Life, liberty, and the pursuit of happiness (when happiness is not at the expense of others) must be protected for even "the least of these." Whenever Christians speak from this motive, regardless of their opinion, I need to listen.

I applaud any effort to respond politically when the needs of the least are being ignored. Conservatives may support the death penalty, but they cannot deny it is inordinately imposed upon poor minorities and is often unjust. Liberals may oppose the pro-life position, but they must acknowledge that if people believe an unborn child is one of the least, they are compelled to do what they can to protect that child. We can argue about these issues, but to suggest Christians shouldn't work against what they consider evil and oppressive is ridiculous. Of course, there are proper and improper political avenues for responding to what we believe to be inappropriate.

Paul Hill, a pastor and an antiabortionist, gunned down a doctor as he walked from his office. He defended his actions as divinely inspired. He was avenging the murder of innocents and protecting the helpless. His parting words, before his execution, were that he had no regrets and that he expected a hero's welcome in heaven. Though clear about his love for unborn children, Paul Hill was vague about how his actions fulfilled the command to love our enemy.

Loving our enemies is a political command. We are not given permission to kill them. We are not even given permission to demonize our political foes. We are not allowed to ignore their opinions or malign their motives. When we do so, we reveal our desire to control and manipulate rather than learn and grow. Loving our enemies means respecting those with differing political views, listening to their perspectives, and seeking common ground.

The command to "do to others what we would have them do to us" is a political litmus test. If I would not want a Muslim to impair or deny my religious freedom, I am compelled to respect and defend the rights of Muslims. This is why the separation of church and state was so important to the founders of the United States. In fairness, when they established these constraints, they were worried about one branch of Christianity holding power. However, in a pluralistic world, this philosophy is especially important. Gracious politics creates the space for religious expression while opposing religious oppression. It allows us to explore ways to apply the principles of Jesus.

I won't pretend this is easy. My younger brother, a Republican, and I almost always take opposing positions on any issue. There was a time when I understood my task as one of correcting his misconceptions and convincing him of my opinion. I am learning to listen. He too cares about this world. He wants it to be a good place for himself and his family. He cares about people. Recently, he asked me, "If they put you and me in a room and asked us to settle all the world's problems, do you think we could do it?"

I answered, "Yes, but not without compromise. We'd have to be flexible. We'd have to be willing to adopt a solution we could both live with." I believe what he and I could accomplish is possible for the human race. Extremely difficult, but possible. What makes it possible is a commitment to relationship, recognizing everyone as a brother or sister, realizing we've been put on the earth and asked to solve its problems.

Gracious politics will be gentle, seeking ways to move forward together rather than leaving anyone behind. It will be humble, recognizing every political opinion is just that—an opinion. It will be open, listening to a great variety of viewpoints before making a decision. It will be compassionate, always focusing on ways to improve the lives of all persons. It won't be easy.

A belief in the salvation of all people eliminates one obstacle—the assumption that our destiny depends on being on the right side of every political issue. We can limit our disagreements to the issues. I don't have to fear for the souls of those who think differently. I don't have to warn them of hell. God is pleased when we strive to create a better world, even when our solutions are simplistic, incomplete, or completely wrong.

We must honestly and humbly share whatever insights, beliefs, and experiences mold our opinions. We must listen carefully to each other, reading between the lines, discerning the desires of our hearts. We must see politics as more like making love and less like fighting a war. The only way we can come to any consensus on the issues of our day is if we are willing to be gracious.

Political Issues

You'd never know he was a rapist and a murderer. Robby is a quiet little man who serves as a chapel clerk in a prison I visit. He's humble, gentle, and well liked by other prisoners and staff. He's had years of therapy and can talk freely about what he did. "I did a terrible thing. There is no excuse. I deserved to spend the past forty years in prison."

It took years for him to accept his responsibility—even more years to forgive himself. Sometime during his imprisonment, he encountered God and allowed God to transform him. Now he's sixty-five years old and worried the parole board might release him. Where would he go? What would he do? His family is gone, and the world has changed.

Ironically, if Robby had committed his crime today, he would be sitting on death row. But, in the 1960s, when Robby was convicted, the death penalty wasn't an option. Instead, he spent the past forty years changing. I'm grateful for that mercy. In my opinion, capital punishment is an ungracious act. It is punitive rather than redemptive. It ends a life prematurely. I believe we should end this practice, but I know many good people disagree with me.

My brother would remind me Robby ended a woman's life prematurely. He's right. What Robby did was heinous.

Conservatives speak of the biblical distinction between murder, taking an innocent life, and punishment, taking a life for a life. There is a difference. Robby's crime demanded a severe response. Finding a balance between the need for justice and the command of grace isn't easy.

However, in my opinion, the command of Jesus is clear. We are called beyond a life for a life, an eye for an eye, a tooth for a tooth. Jesus taught a new ethic—one in which his disciples overcome evil with good. The early Church was clear on this command. Paul writes, "Do not repay anyone evil for evil, but take thought for what is noble in the sight of all" (Romans 12:17). My brother doesn't argue with this. He just doesn't like it. I sympathize. Tit for tat comes so much easier to me than grace. This is why I'm so suspicious of retributive justice. We find it so attractive.

I don't believe we should kill Robby. I think we should forgive him. Though crime must be punished, I can't imagine Jesus's pulling the lever on an electric chair. I can imagine Jesus's sending criminals to prison, where he would visit them often. Republicans are right to emphasize accountability and consequence. Democrats are right to counter with the need for reformation. A gracious political position must value both concerns. But forgiveness, I think, rather than public execution, is the nobler path.

I am not an opponent of long prison sentences. I've discovered prison can be a gracious place—where men and women are allowed the time and space to deal with their problems and accept the consequences of their behavior. My friend Mike has spent the past twenty-three years in prison. When his last appeal was denied, he stood in a chapel service and said, "I can learn and grow and serve God anyplace." Mike told me prison was the best thing to happen to him—without it he was destined to destroy many other lives, including his own.

Ironically, I would feel much safer if Mike were released than the many people who walk out the doors of prison, without remorse and demonstrating no real transformation, simply because their sentence has ended. The idea that a certain number of years satisfy a debt is to misunderstand how crime and violence damage relationships. Repentance and restitution, not imprisonment, restore relationship. Gracious politics would take seriously and literally the names we use for prisons—reformatories and penitentiaries. There is nothing ungracious about being tough on crime if we are also compassionate toward criminals.

Gracious politics would also focus its energies on the causes of crime—poverty, abusive parenting, and a lack of education. We know the factors most likely to lead to crime. It costs about twenty-five thousand dollars a year to incarcerate someone. It would be politically and economically wiser to spend this money elsewhere. Killing a person does nothing to remedy the situations that create killers.

Capital punishment is not the only issue to which grace speaks. I am mystified how some can defend death in one setting and decry it in another. I have never understood how liberals can protest when a person is executed, but mock those picketing an abortion clinic, or how someone can be pro-life while supporting capital punishment. Gracious politics defends the rights of all people, even the unborn and the criminal.

In my opinion, abortion is often an ungracious act. I believe we should limit this practice, though I know many good people disagree. But I wonder if in legalizing abortion, we've valued freedom over the sanctity of human life. The rationale is similar to our justification for war, in which our freedoms supersede the right of our "enemy" to live. Whenever we value one life over another, we undermine the sanctity of life. Calling an unborn child a fetus does not negate his or her worth, just as calling others the "enemy" doesn't diminish their value.

What makes the topic of abortion so painfully difficult is that our understandings of grace collide. Though it is ungracious to take a human life, it is equally ungracious to demand a woman care for and continue a life she feels ill-equipped to nurture. A commitment to gracious politics requires us to create systems of support that assist women in the daunting task of raising a human being, especially when men can so easily (and often legally) evade their responsibilities to nurture and provide for their children.

In a gracious world, abortions would be rare and always the lesser to two evils. When a fourteen-year-old who'd been molested by her stepfather over a period of several years became pregnant, I supported her decision to abort the child. This young girl had been traumatized enough. Forcing her to carry the child would have been victimizing her again.

On the other hand, in my experience, most abortions are far less complicated. For many, it is an attempt to escape the consequences of bad decisions. For others, it is simply self-absorption. Many middle- and upper-class women don't want an unplanned pregnancy to impair their freedom. Though I've heard the arguments about protecting poor women from the burdens of supporting more children, I've never found this compelling. In the inner-city neighborhoods I've lived in, women rarely had abortions. They, usually for the wrong reasons, had babies.

This reality is why I'm also critical of the pro-life movement. Too often, the people protesting in front of abortion clinics are the most resistant to giving away birth control in the schools and providing tax support for poor children. Though it is ungracious to take an unborn child's life, it is equally ungracious not to value a toddler's life. We cannot have it both ways—if all children are precious, they are precious when they become hungry infants, rebellious teenagers, or convicted criminals. Gracious politics accepts our responsibility not to simply protect life, but to commit ourselves to seeing every life fulfilled and abundant.

Since gracious politics calls us to see every life blessed, I can no longer oppose same-gender marriage. I do understand the strong reaction of many Christians to this idea. I once found homosexuality abhorrent and the idea of same-sex marriages outrageous. That was when I was convinced sexual orientation was a choice and homosexuality a perversion. This opinion was easy to maintain when I didn't know any homosexuals, but impossible to retain when my prejudices were confronted with reality.

I was born into a large family, with three brothers and a sister. Though I was the first to marry, my siblings soon followed. Only one of my brothers remained single, showing no interest in women. For years, we teased him about being a bachelor, unaware of how painful our taunts must have been. The truth was my brother had a mate. We just hadn't met him.

When my grandfather died and my entire family gathered after the funeral, my brother found the courage to come out of the closet. He didn't demand my acceptance, but I gave it anyway. He is my brother and I love him. I also realized my experience with my brother challenged the belief that homosexuality was a choice. He had always been different. Now I knew why. The idea he'd suddenly decided to be gay was silly. The assumption that his lifestyle made him evil was preposterous.

Many Christians consider homosexuality a sinful choice. Such behavior is so alien they cannot even imagine it. Yet the very fact I can't imagine being homosexual should imply that my brother can't imagine being heterosexual. It isn't a choice. It is how God made him. My responsibility is not to change him, but to understand him.

I soon had that opportunity. Several weeks later, I met his partner of nearly fifteen years. Watching them interact

with one another over a period of several days, I was reminded, again and again, of my own relationship with my
wife. They too were happy and fulfilled with each other.
How could I deny my brother the same happiness I treasured? Sometimes they were more gracious in their relationship than my wife and I were in ours. Was I willing to
learn from their relationship?

In my opinion, it is ungracious to deny another person a
satisfaction or right I demand for myself. I must do for others what I would have them do for me. What I expected
from my brother was that he would love and support me
and my spouse. I could do nothing less for him. Neither
could I deny him and his partner the joys and privileges my
wife and I enjoyed.

I don't understand the insistence by some that this is a
moral, rather than civil rights, issue. On the other hand, I
can understand the wisdom of creating two types of rela-
tional recognition—civil unions and marriages. Civil unions
would become a function of the government—a means of
valuing and regulating the legal privileges and responsibilities in both heterosexual and homosexual relationships.
Marriages, which imply divine blessing, would remain a religious ceremony for those who choose it and whose communities of faith are willing to extend such a blessing.

Gracious politics does not advocate rights for some that
it denies to men and women of other convictions. It does not
seek advantage for one special interest over another. It does

not value the worth of one person over another. Instead, it works to create a world where we can optimize the goodness of each life while recognizing our responsibility to the common good.

This is the proper task for politics. Religion reminds us of what is important. Politics formally establishes these values in communities, states, and nations. When religion calls us to love our neighbors, politics gives our neighbors a voice and a vote. When religion calls us to love our enemies, politics keeps us from mistreating or harming our enemies. When religion says to treat others graciously, politics must seek to offer this grace to all.

Believing in the salvation of all people has tempered every aspect of my life, but perhaps none more than my political views. There was a day when I believed there was only one way. Politics was about manipulating others into accepting my worldview. It was a battle with only one possible winner. I no longer believe that. What I hope for is a world where grace abounds and the only parties that matter are the ones we celebrate together.

1. Tony Campolo, *Ideas for Social Action* (Grand Rapids, MI: Zondervan, 1983), p. 11. Campolo is one of those Christians capable of being both orthodox and radical.
2. John Howard Yoder, *The Politics of Jesus* (Grand Rapids, MI: Eerdmans, 1972), p. 62.
3. Ralph Reed, *Active Faith: How Christians Are Changing the Soul of American Politics* (New York: Free Press, 1996), p. 255. A thorough and insightful history and analysis of the conservative Christian political

movement from one of its key proponents. Reed is remarkably candid and self-critical.

4. Frederick Clarkson, "Christian Reconstructionism: Theocratic Dominionism Gains Influence," *The Public Eye* 8, nos. 1–2 (March, June 1994). Clarkson's analysis might be ignored as leftist critique, if not for the fact that Ralph Reed is critical of this same group and theology.

8

Money and Grace

My hands shook the first time I preached on the salvation of all people. I'd previously admitted my doubts about hell and Satan and had been fired for expressing my misgivings. Now, many years later, I was pastoring a congregation where I was liked and respected. This finally gave me the courage to preach that God would save all, though I did it with fear and trembling.

Some of my hesitation was personal. I was still exploring the many ramifications of altering my theology, uncertain how to voice what I sensed to be true. But not all my indecision was as noble. There were also economic considerations. I didn't want to be fired again.

This was not paranoia. The week after I preached on the salvation of all, two elders in my congregation visited my office to ask me to return to the faith, or else. They did this tearfully, concerned for my soul. When it became clear they couldn't persuade me with scriptures and theological arguments, one of them said, "Don't you realize you're destroying your career and threatening your livelihood?"

I wasn't certain I was destroying my career, but he was clearly threatening my livelihood. I said, "Do you really think I would have stayed at this inner-city church and accepted my meager salary if prestige and money were my incentives?" I found his assumptions about my priorities much more disturbing than our theological differences. Unfortunately, I've found his attitude far too common.

Only a few weeks later, I was speaking with a publishing friend. I was telling him of my desire to write a book about God's grace for all people. He responded, "That's great! There's a lot of money in grace." Though he meant his words as an encouragement, I found it troubling so many thought economics were the ultimate incentive. Was every decision always determined by the bottom line?

I'm not naive. I understand the necessity of an economic system. I know money, as a means of exchange, is morally neutral. Unfortunately, I also know how often money becomes an end rather than a means. I've learned this from personal experience. I am not immune to greed.

My first royalty check was the largest sum of money I'd ever had. I immediately thought of a dozen personal uses for the money. It was so easy to justify rewarding myself, to allow my desires to increase with my resources, and to forget why I wrote. It wasn't for the money. I didn't need the money. My life was comfortable before I received that check. Regardless, my first thoughts were completely self-absorbed.

In the years since, I have tried, sometimes unsuccessfully, to resist skimming off the top. I've funneled many of those dollars into efforts to make the world a more gracious place. The profits from books proclaiming God's concern for all persons should profit as many people as possible. Yet each time I receive a check, I realize how easily I can be compromised.

I am not alone. Religion often bows to economics. As a pastor, I can't count the times a gracious proposal was rejected by the church because it wasn't financially prudent. I am equally amazed how often we've found money for new carpet or padded pews. In decision making, there was an angel on one shoulder and a banker on the other. Too often, we listened to the banker.

This is especially disturbing when we claim to follow Jesus. Jesus may have been ambiguous when it came to politics, but he didn't mince words when it came to economics. He said, "No one can serve two masters; for a slave will either hate the one and love the other, or be devoted to the one and despise the other. You cannot serve God and wealth" (Matthew 6:24). The marriage of religion and wealth is a marriage made in hell.

Religion and Wealth

I spent many years serving a church in the inner city. It was a small middle-class congregation in a much poorer neighborhood. The parishioners were good people who could be very generous. When I became pastor, they told me the annual Easter offering would often exceed five thousand dollars. Impressed, I spent several weeks before the January meeting coming up with good uses for this offering.

At the meeting, I stood and outlined several options—a program digging wells in Africa, an effort to build better housing in the inner city, a neighborhood summer program for youth. My suggestions were met with icy stares or confused expressions. After I finished, another man suggested the church refrigerator, which still worked, needed to be replaced. In a matter of seconds, the church voted to purchase a new refrigerator.

Later, I learned the Easter offering had always been used to make improvements and add comforts to the church building. They'd celebrated the good news of the resurrection and God's love for all people by buying themselves gifts. This was especially hard to swallow when a few months later our church couldn't find the funds for a youth outreach program.

I wish this example were the exception rather than the rule, but I've discovered most Christians are not very generous. A recent study found we give only 1.8 percent of our income to charity. This includes all we give to our churches—much of which benefits us rather than the poor and oppressed. When I finally challenged the priorities of our Easter offering, one man warned, "If people don't see a personal benefit, they're much less likely to give." He was right. When we collected for a social ministry, our donations went down 50 percent. That charitable giving is tax deductible suggests even altruism must benefit us personally.

Unfortunately, when religion becomes the servant of economics, religious institutions become brothels, soliciting customers with powder and blush, selling our wares to the highest bidder. When churches are funded by Bingo nights or lure people with coffee and gift shops, they appeal to selfishness and self-indulgence. When we Christians donate a pittance to God and lavish the remainder on ourselves, we become spiritual embezzlers. Rather than redeeming wealth, we are corrupted by it.

Jesus continually warned his disciples of wealth's insidious power. He said, "It is easier for a camel to go through the eye of a needle than for someone who is rich to enter the kingdom of God" (Matthew 19:24). He proclaimed, "Blessed are you who are poor, for yours is the kingdom of God. . . . Woe to you who are rich, for you have received your consolation" (Luke 6:20, 24). Jesus told one rich person, "Sell everything you have and give to the poor, and you will have treasure in heaven. Then come, follow me" (Luke 18:22, NIV). He gave his disciples these instructions when he sent them into the world to minister: "You received without payment; give without payment" (Matthew 10:8).

These cautions and commands were not solely for religious leaders—they were for every disciple. Paul warns: "The love of money is a root of all kinds of evil, and in their eagerness to be rich some have wandered away from the faith and pierced themselves with many pains" (1 Timothy 6:10). It is not homosexuality that has eroded "family values" in our country. It is unchallenged and unbridled materialism. Greed twists our motives and alters our priorities.

Wealth and the desire for wealth are jealous taskmasters. They demand our full allegiance and complete attention. To be wealthy requires self-absorption. This single-minded commitment to satisfying and advancing our own needs allows us to ignore the legitimate needs of others. We don't mean to be cruel. We simply don't have the time and energy to focus on others. Some of us may respond if we're made to feel guilty. Others may react if there is some personal benefit. But we resist seeing the needs of others as our responsibility.

Economic inequality, rather than being a blight on society, becomes a measure of success. Our worth is measured in dollars. The poor are worth less. We justify our inordinate portion of the economic pie as a sign of personal achievement. Horatio Alger wrote stories of the poor pulling themselves up by their bootstraps and becoming millionaires. We forget his books were fiction. Stories of the poor rising to wealth and privilege make the newspapers because such stories qualify as news—they are rare and noteworthy. When we identify wealth as a reward rather than a responsibility, we kill compassion and grace.

If wealth and the desire for wealth actually brought happiness and security, they might be defensible. Unfortunately, there is no correlation between wealth and fulfillment. Economic excess, where more is never enough, often comes at the cost of impoverishing our spirits and others' bodies.

Thousands of years ago, the writer of Ecclesiastes confessed, "Whatever my eyes desired I did not keep from them; I kept my heart from no pleasure. . . . Then I considered all my hands had done and the toil I had spent in doing it, and again, all was vanity and a chasing after wind" (Ecclesiastes 2:10 11). Jesus told the story of a man who reaped a great harvest and built more silos to hold his wealth. God says, "You fool! This very night your life is being demanded of you. And the things you have prepared, whose will they be?" (Luke 12:20). The one who dies with the most toys dies selfish.

Thomas Merton said, "A happiness that is sought for ourselves alone can never be found: for a happiness that is diminished by being shared is not big enough to make us happy."[1] Wealth does not give us the happiness we desire. Often, our wealth makes us less secure and satisfied. The more we have, the more we risk losing. Buying a bigger house means less freedom to move, to change jobs, to be generous. My father often says, "It's not how much you own; it's how much owns you." We become enslaved to the very things we thought would make us free.

Unfortunately, wealth and the desire for wealth not only damage our souls; they also lead to the oppression of others. Wealth makes us ungracious. I ignore the environmental, societal, and human price of maintaining my level of affluence. So what if Styrofoam is filling our landfills, so long as it's convenient? So what if the tax abatement for the new stadium robs inner-city schools, so long as we are entertained? So what if children in overseas sweatshops made our name-brand clothes, so long as we are fashionable? We kill people in order to accumulate trinkets.

Those with more justify their abundance by implying those with less are morally deficient—lazy or wicked. Those with more must guard what they've hoarded from those who have less. When visiting Honduras, I noticed every place of affluence—nice homes, the bank, Wendy's restaurant—had a guard with an M-16 standing outside. When I commented on this to a Honduran, he pointed out the United States does the same thing. We simply hide the weapons guarding our affluence in missile silos and nuclear submarines.

He went on to point out that, though he appreciated the efforts of our mission team to bring clean water to a mountain village, he hoped I would return home aware of the responsibilities of being a North American Christian. From those to whom much is given much is required. Did my religion justify and sanctify my affluence, or did it challenge me to work for economic equality?

Christianity has often refused to heed the clear call of Jesus to economic equality. We've made charity—the bandaging of wounds—our focus and ignored how the sharp edges of our economic system tear and rip the poor. We give food to inner-city food pantries and fail to address the practice of the price gouging that plagues inner-city grocery stores. We loan people money for rent and utilities and ignore how rent-to-own and check-cashing businesses charge exorbitant interest. We open soup kitchens and homeless shelters while applauding cuts in social programs and demanding lower taxes. We sponsor children in impoverished countries and tolerate the austere demands of the World Bank that contribute to their never-ending desperation. We define missionaries as those who tell people about Jesus rather than those who heal the sick, feed the poor, and set the captives free.

Religious dualism is especially vulnerable to confusion about wealth when affluence is often preached as a sign of God's blessing. Even gracious words become twisted. Jesus said, "If you then, who are evil, know how to give good gifts to your children, how much more will your Father in heaven give good things to those who ask him!" (Matthew 7:11). I have heard this scripture quoted repeatedly by preachers who believe Christians, as children of the King, deserve more good things than others. When we divide the world into the deserving children of God and the unworthy children of Satan, we absolve ourselves of any responsibility to care for non-Christians.

A few years ago, a hurricane smashed into Honduras, destroying whole villages, demolishing roads and bridges, and wiping neighborhoods off the sides of mountains. Thousands died, and tens of thousands were left with nothing. In the midst of that disaster, our church joined others in raising funds, collecting food and clothing, and shipping trailer loads of supplies to that beleaguered nation. Many people were generous. However, one man's reply to our request for help was especially troubling. He said, "Why should we help them when there are plenty of our own who need food and clothing?"

I've often heard such sentiments. What they suggest is that those in other lands and other faiths aren't "our own" or our responsibility. The world is divided into spheres of concern, with us in the center. We care for ourselves first, our family second, our neighbors next, our fellow citizens if possible, and those foreigners with whatever scraps we have left. One missionary told me of receiving a large box of used tea bags from a church. Charity is what we do with our leftovers.

This hierarchy of compassion is largely dependent upon a dualistic view of the world, one divided into "us" and "them." "Us" is those living in our country or belonging to our religion. "Them" is everyone else—strangers, foreigners, infidels, and pagans. In one fell swoop, we justify our affluence, excuse ourselves from responsibility, and sanctify wealth as the sign of God's favor. Blessed are the rich, for the kingdom of God belongs to them.

Of course, that isn't what Jesus said. In his parable of the rich man and Lazarus, the rich man ends up in hell (Luke 16:19–31). I know this story well. Whenever I speak of the salvation of all, someone will cite this passage as proof of hell and damnation. He or she will point out that Jesus clearly said the rich man was in hell and, by focusing on the scenery of this parable, miss its point—those who spend their lives living extravagantly while others starve outside their gates disappoint God. In cultures, then and now, where divine favor and wealth are seen as synonymous, this parable is a radical challenge.

This passage also clarifies what Jesus thought of poverty. He pictures the dogs licking the wounds of Lazarus while the rich man feasts. Jesus may have called the poor blessed, but he never glamorized poverty. He wanted the needs of the poor alleviated. When people were hungry, he fed them. When they were ill, he cared for them. He told his disciples to give to those who asked and share with those who were in need. Jesus was critical of the wealthy not because poverty is noble, but because economic oppression offends God.

Jesus was one in a long line of biblical voices challenging the tendency of religion to justify ungracious economics. The prophets were united in their disappointment with the participation of the religious in economic injustice. Ezekiel said, "Ah, you shepherds of Israel who have been feeding yourselves! Should not the shepherds feed the sheep? You eat the fat, you clothe yourselves with the wool, you slaughter the fatlings; but you do not feed the sheep. You have not strengthened the weak, you have not healed the sick, you have not bound up the injured, you have not brought back the strayed, you have not sought the lost, but with force and harshness you have ruled them" (Ezekiel 34:2–4). Ezekiel recognized how often religion becomes a means of economic gain and self-absorption rather than a critique of economic inequality.

Clarence Jordan tells the story of a church in Florida that spent forty thousand dollars on a "Flowers of the Bible" garden, full of the roses of Sharon and the lilies of the valley. Jordan said: "In that same city, I visited a day care center with approximately seventy-five little flowers in it. They were black flowers. Their playground, I give you my word, was hardly as big as a garage. They had no equipment. And here these idiotic 'Christians' spent forty thousand dollars on exotic flowers and not one dime on God's little flowers."[2]

Gracious religion spends money on the right flowers. It calls us away from personal comfort, wealth, and security as the purpose of life. We consider the needs of others as equal to our own. We are called to do more than provide the poor with handouts. We are to take their hands and lift them from despair. The goal is not to diminish our lives, but to see that all lives are blessed. When religion doesn't temper our selfishness and remind us of our responsibilities to others, religion is worthless, an exercise in self-justification.

I don't pretend systemic change can come easily and quickly, but we cannot be satisfied as long as children are starving to death. I'm not suggesting we abandon acts of charity, but we can never substitute these acts for economic equality. Gracious religion challenges every idea or system that encourages us to ignore or diminish the needs of "the least of these." Ungracious economics must end. Fortunately, Jesus didn't simply offer a condemnation of wealth and a critique of economics. He also offered an alternative approach.

The Economics of Jesus

"Share everything with your brother. Do not say, 'It is private property.'" This isn't the rhetoric of the *Communist Manifesto* or *The Mother Earth Catalog*. This is a line from the *Didache,* an early Christian document used to prepare novices for baptism. The *Didache* was such a respected teaching it was nearly included in the biblical canon. This line may have been its undoing. Religion has long resisted the command to be universally concerned, especially when this concern comes with a price tag.

I understand this tendency. Whenever someone asks me to respond to a need, I have to overcome a long litany of mental excuses. I don't know enough about the person's situation to give wisely. He or she might not use the money appropriately. I'm already giving to other causes. These may all be legitimate considerations, but I sense my deeper motivation—I want a rationale for keeping my money. I don't like Jesus's command to "Give to everyone who begs from you, and do not refuse anyone who wants to borrow from you" (Matthew 5:42). This seems irresponsible rather than gracious. Of course, Jesus may have suggested such radical generosity precisely because of how much we resist our responsibility to care for others.

When a rich young man asked Jesus, "What must I do to inherit eternal life?" Jesus suggested he keep the commandments, but the man wasn't satisfied. Like many of us, he sensed there must be more to religion than keeping the rules. The Bible says, "Jesus, looking at him, loved him and said, 'You lack one thing; go, sell what you own, and give the money to the poor, and you will have treasure in heaven; then come, follow me'" (Mark 10:21). Unfortunately, that man found the call to extravagance too costly. "When he heard this, he was shocked and went away grieving, for he had many possessions" (Mark 10:22).

We shouldn't be too hard on this man. I suspect if Jesus were to suggest this to most American Christians, we too would grieve. Or we'd do what we do with all difficult commands—we'd rationalize and minimize. When I was growing up, we were told Jesus didn't mean we should sell everything. He meant we should be *willing* to sell everything. It was the attitude, not the action, that mattered.

Donald Kraybill, in his book *The Upside Down Kingdom,* says: "Jesus, according to this view, was concerned with the private matters of the inner life. He cared primarily about character, attitudes, motives, emotions, personality traits. Hence the ethics of Jesus apply only to inner feelings which have little impact on others."[3] In adopting such a view, we miss why Jesus challenged the rich young man. His problem wasn't theological. He knew the right answers. His sin was inaction.

James asked these same questions of the early Church. He said, "What good is it, my brothers and sisters, if you say you have faith, but do not have works? Can faith save you?" (James 2:14). Traditional Christianity has usually asserted we are saved by faith. James didn't agree. He said, "If a brother or a sister is naked and lacks daily food, and one of you says to them, 'Go in peace; keep warm and eat your fill,' and yet you do not supply their bodily needs, what is the good of that? So faith, by itself, if it has no works, is dead" (James 2:15–17). Salvation—turning from self-absorption and toward right relationship with God and others—is demonstrated in generosity.

Jesus made this clear when he visited a tax collector named Zacchaeus. He went to his house and had dinner with him. We don't know what Jesus said to Zacchaeus, but we know how Zacchaeus responded. Zacchaeus announced, "Look, half of my possessions, Lord, I will give to the poor; and if I have defrauded anyone of anything, I will pay back four times as much." Then Jesus said to him, "Today salvation has come to this house" (Luke 19:8–9).

Years ago, when the famine in Somalia was at its height, I sat down with my family to eat a pizza. We had the television on, and we saw emaciated men, women, and children eating gruel from metal cups. For some, even this meager ration came too late. One clip showed bodies piled like sticks.

As powerful as these images were, it was an interview that brought me to tears. In the interview, a father, holding a naked child whose stomach was bloated by malnutrition, had already lost several children to starvation. He spoke of his grief, of his desperation, of his hopelessness. He appealed directly to the camera for help. A father myself, I experienced the empathy so crucial to grace.

The end of the program asked for a donation of twenty-five dollars to feed a family of four for one month. As I sat there, my appetite disappearing, I realized we'd spent twenty-five dollars to feed our family of four one meal. I picked up the phone, as much out of guilt as grace, and made my pledge. Salvation came to my house.

That night, as never before, I realized another ramification of believing in the salvation of all persons. If they will be my brothers and sisters in heaven, I must treat them as family right now, whether they live down the street or across the globe. The salvation of all can't remain theological speculation. It must inspire a new way of thinking about our responsibility as citizens of this world. If God loves all of us equally, then a world of vast inequalities grieves God. If I claim to be godly, these injustices must concern me.

Believing in the salvation of every person means being universally concerned. We abandon those distinctions that so easily allow us to be hostile or apathetic. My response to starving children isn't dependent on whether they're black or white, Christian or non-Christian, American or foreign. Their being human makes them my responsibility.

The economic system of Jesus can be summarized with one word: Give. The *Didache* taught new Christians to share generously and to abandon an obsession with personal possessions because Jesus considered extravagant generosity a sign of faithfulness. Jesus said, "Give, and it will be given to you. A good measure, pressed down, shaken together, running over, will be put in your lap; for the measure you give will be the measure you get back" (Luke 6:38). In the economy of God, we become rich not by hoarding our wealth, but by giving it away.

We are invited to do something outrageous, counter to what we've been taught and reasonable only if we have faith in God. We are to give away what we have, confident our generosity will produce abundance for all. I think this happened when Jesus fed the five thousand (Matthew 14:13–21). I don't think God miraculously created more food. The problems of our world are seldom because of a lack of resources. It is unequal distribution that impoverishes many.

When Jesus told his disciples to share their meager resources with the crowd, they thought him irresponsible. Yet this generosity inspired many others to share what they were hoarding. In the end, there were twelve baskets of leftovers. Anyone who has attended a church potluck dinner should recognize this reality—when we are generous, everyone is blessed.

This was the experience of the early Church. In Acts, we read, "All who believed were together and had all things in common; they would sell their possessions and goods and distribute the proceeds to all, as any had need" (Acts

2:44–45). Though many churches argue for a return to New Testament Christianity, I've yet to hear them suggest we model ourselves after this aspect of the early Church. Some want to speak in tongues or heal. Others want prophetic preaching and evangelism. No one seems interested in economic equality.

In fairness, the early Church soon abandoned this priority. This does not mean such a commitment is impossible. It was, and is, difficult. Paul, writing to a church in Corinth that resisted this challenge, said, "I do not mean that there should be relief for others and pressure on you, but it is a question of a fair balance between your present abundance and their need, so that their abundance may be for your need, in order that there may be a fair balance" (2 Corinthians 8:13–14). The goal is not our impoverishment, but bringing about equity. If my brother or sister is hungry, I don't need to pray about it. I need to feed him or her.

Of course, the old adage, when it is not an excuse for inactivity, rings true: feed a man a fish, you meet his needs for a day; teach a man to fish and you meet his needs for a lifetime. We are called to more than personal generosity. We are called to challenge ungracious economic systems that deny people the right and resources to fish.

Ungracious Economics

I live a few blocks from one of the largest health-care companies in the nation—Anthem Blue Cross and Blue Shield. It also happens to provide my health insurance. This dynamic has made me particularly sensitive to a growing trend in American corporations—the erosion of social responsibility.

Recently, the headlines in the *Indianapolis Star* announced that the top five executives at Anthem would receive $90 million in bonuses. The Anthem CEO, Larry Glasscock, received a $42 million bonus. This was on top of their annual salaries of nearly $15 million.[4] This was especially disturbing when my family was one of the many who received letters informing us that, "because of the high cost of health care," our premiums would be raised again.

It is important to understand the history of Anthem. It is one of the fastest-growing corporations in the world. Most of its growth has come from swallowing up not-for-profit insurance companies. It has aggressively marketed its stock and generously rewarded its stockholders. Indeed, I discovered when I visited its Web site that when it mentions "customers," it isn't talking about the sick and diseased, whom it insures. Its customers are the stockholders. Though it claims its goal is to provide affordable health care, it clearly is more interested in making money.

In fairness, Anthem's strategy isn't much different from that of Enron, Worldcom, or Global Crossing. Greed has run rampant in recent years. The problem with Anthem is its profits are being made at the expense of the sick and diseased. Health care has become one more product, and insurance companies aren't the only culprits.

William Boyer, author of *Myth America,* says: "United States medical costs as a percentage of the GNP are the highest of any nation and we also have the lowest level of insurance coverage of any industrialized nation. A significant cost is bypass surgery, which is unnecessary except in unusual cases."[5] Boyer suggests the primary factor for doing bypass surgery is not health—many studies find no increase in longevity—but profit. Surgeons make money.

Of course, making money is the American way. Our economic system is built on the assumption that self-interest, self-gratification, and greed are the most effective engines for economic vitality. Adam Smith, the father of capitalism, said, "It is not from the benevolence of the butcher, the brewer, or the baker that we expect our dinner, but from their regard to their own interest. We address ourselves, not to their humanity but to their self-love, and never talk to them of our own necessities but of their advantages. Nobody but a beggar chooses to depend chiefly upon the benevolence of his fellow-citizens."[6]

Capitalism assumes the worst about us: we will act only when it is in our self-interest. We cannot be expected to be benevolent or gracious. We may talk of being civilized, but when it comes to economics, it is the law of the jungle—eat or be eaten. Corporations are not designed to promote the common good, but to fill the pockets of a select few. People become objects—consumers, resources, assets, or liabilities. Profit becomes the only measure of success. Capital is used to create more wealth rather than a better world.

The proponents of the free market will protest that capitalism offers everyone the opportunity to succeed. They argue that regulation inhibits human freedom. Unfortunately, they assume a level playing field. A free market can't succeed when there are also great disparities in military and political power. Everyone is not equally free to prosper when a few control all the resources and the avenues to using these resources. In Honduras, every time a government would suggest the fruit companies, who paid their workers a pittance, should be nationalized, the United States intervened militarily. Each intervention was justified as a defense of freedom—the freedom of the fruit companies to increase their profits. Any economic system founded on selfishness and maintained by violence is deeply flawed.

Capitalism is not beyond redemption. Democracy, which upholds the inalienable rights of all people to life, liberty, and the pursuit of happiness, must temper the excesses of capitalism. Capitalism may be self-absorbed, but democracy reminds us of the common good. In a democratic society, corporations gain legitimacy not by how much money they make, but by how they contribute to the lives, liberty, and happiness of people.

Corporations have become far too powerful. In 1864, Abraham Lincoln warned, "I see in the near future a crisis approaching that unnerves me and causes me to tremble for the safety of my country. As the result of the War, corporations have been enthroned. . . . An era of corruption in high places will follow, and the money power of the country will endeavor to prolong its reign by working upon the prejudices of the people . . . until wealth is aggregated in a few hands . . . and the Republic is destroyed."[7]

With globalization, even democratic societies have less and less ability to check corporate arrogance. How do we encourage corporations to be environmentally or socially responsible when they can simply move their factories to a nation where they are allowed to pollute and abuse workers without restraint? Corporate power threatens democracy. It threatens our world.

Yet corporations are made up of people—many of whom are gracious and compassionate. Our task is to allow generosity and responsibility to become as valued as profit in the corporate world. Rabbi Michael Lerner suggests:

In economics, I'd like to see a Social Responsibility Amendment to the U.S. Constitution: Corporations with incomes of over $30 million a year would have to get a new corporate charter every ten years, and

they'd get one only if they could prove to a jury of
ordinary citizens that they had a satisfactory record
of social responsibility. . . . It would suddenly be possible for decent people in corporations to do what
they are now kept from doing: acting in the best interest of the human race.[8]

There was a time in my life when I would have presented Larry Glasscock and the executives at Anthem as evidence of the inherent evil of the capitalist system. I don't
believe that anymore. Capitalism, communism, and social-
ism have all had their scandals. The problem isn't in the systems—it's in our understanding of what brings joy.

Some men and women think joy is in having or controlling far more resources than they can ever possibly use. Others experience satisfaction in sharing their resources with
those who have less. This division isn't limited to men and
women in places of power. It runs down Wall Street, through
the streets and roads of the United States, and into the alleys
of the inner city. Even at homeless shelters some find happiness in what they possess and others experience the joy of
sharing the little they have with those around them.

A gracious economic system is not created by compulsion
or command, but by a change of heart. As long as we remain
concerned only for ourselves, or for a portion of our country or
world, we will be able to justify economic inequality. When
our joy is in seeing debts forgiven, the hungry fed, the sick
healed, and the poor blessed, then we shall experience jubilee.

Jubilee Economics

Smack in the middle of all the dos and don'ts of Leviticus, in chapter 25, is an odd command to celebrate a year of jubilee. The idea was simple. Every fifty years, the nation of Israel was to remember that joy isn't found in how much you have. The people were reminded of their responsibility to be fair and to provide for the poor.

It was a simple command. Every fifty years, the land returned to its original owners. Those who had grown rich by buying the land of others had to return it to them. Those who had become poor and destitute would have the land they'd lost given back. Debts were forgiven. Everyone, rich or poor, was allowed to start over.

Leviticus defends this command with two comments. First, in verse 17, we are reminded not to take advantage of each other, that with wealth comes power over other people. The year of jubilee was a means of keeping power from settling permanently in a few hands. Second, in verse 23, God reminds those who would complain of the unfairness of such forgiveness: "The land must not be sold permanently, because the land is mine and you are but aliens and my tenants" (NIV). The year of jubilee was designed to remind every person that the earth and all that is in it belongs to the Lord. We are merely stewards of God's possessions.

Before we get too excited about this radical system of debt forgiveness, before we write our senators and suggest we adopt this model, we should know most scholars doubt this command was ever obeyed. Those in power were quick to enact the punishments for those who murdered, lied, committed adultery, or stole from others. They were not nearly as keen on adopting the year of jubilee.

Those in power decided their joy was not in forgiving debts, but in acquiring possessions. This is why hundreds of years later, we find Paul writing the Christians in Corinth, a very wealthy city, and reminding them of the same principles. He asked those who had plenty to supply those who had need. He suggested people shouldn't gather more than they needed or could use. He said, "God loves a cheerful giver" (2 Corinthians 9:7).

Gracious economics happen when we get excited about giving to others, when we take the concept of jubilee seriously. Though I'll admit it's too rare, jubilee happens.

Jacob Shenk was a businessman living in Virginia during the Great Depression. While others were barely making ends meet, Jacob Shenk devised a plan to give poor farmers fertilized eggs and grain to raise chickens, and then bought those chickens back from them to sell to grocery stores. Within a few years, his trucks were crisscrossing Virginia, and he was making thousands of dollars. He became wealthy beyond his dreams.

Fortunately, his fondest dream was to serve God. He resolved to take 90 percent of his profits and return them to charitable causes in the United States and around the world. The IRS, convinced no one could give so much money away, audited him year after year. One year, when profits were especially high, he decided to divide his windfall with all the farmers who worked for him and mailed them all sizable checks. He wanted them to know how much he appreciated their hard work. When Jacob Shenk died tragically in 1950, people from across Virginia, from every stratum of life, celebrated his generosity and goodness. He brought jubilee.[9]

What Jacob Shenk did in the 1930s and 1940s, Bob Thompson did in the 1990s. Bob Thompson spent his whole life building an asphalt company in Michigan. It was hard, hot work—fourteen hour days, six days a week in the summer. He began with a few employees and over the years built the company into the largest road-paving company in the Midwest. But in 1999, he was seventy-two years old and ready to retire. He sold his company for $422 million. He gave much of this money away to charities, but he also demonstrated a jubilee spirit.

In a letter, he notified his employees of his decision to sell the company. His letter explained that he had sold the company to a firm known for its integrity, and it had promised not to lay off any of his workers. That was his first piece of good news. The second announcement was that he was giving $128 million of the purchase price back to his 550 employees. He was giving $2,000 for every year someone had worked for him, and to 80 people who'd been with him from near the beginning—he was giving $1 million apiece.

When his generosity became news, reporters rushed to his home, a humble ranch-style house he'd bought when he first got married, and asked him why he was doing this. His answer was simple: "It brings me joy."

Of course, we don't have to be millionaires to celebrate jubilee. I once pastored an elderly couple, each of whom received a Social Security check. They lived on one check and distributed the other to persons in need. Though they did without many of the things we believe constitute "the good life," it was clear to those who knew them that their lives had a richness and joy few attain.

I know another man who, while sitting in church, heard his pastor challenge the youth of their congregation with the question, "What are you going to do with your life?" Driving home, this middle-aged owner of a successful company heard a radio commercial for the Peace Corps. Recently divorced, he realized he was free to remake his life. He spent two years in Africa going from village to village teaching blacksmithing. When he returned to the States, he built a small home, opened a company in an economically depressed town, and hired people struggling to make ends meet.

I tell you about these people because I want us to understand that the answer to the world's problems is not in passing legislation enacting a year of jubilee. If we did, lawyers would find loopholes long before we got to the fiftieth year. The answer to the inequalities in the world is for men and women like you and me to understand the reasons God commanded such generosity. They are simple and clear. When we live by these principles, we and those around us experience jubilee.

The earth and all that is in it belongs to the Lord. We are only stewards. We are responsible for making certain what belongs to the Lord is equally distributed to his children. Those who gather more should give to those who gather less. If you have two coats, you should give one to someone else. If you have too big a house, you should downsize and use your equity to provide housing opportunities for the poor. If you don't need two cars, you should sell one. If you have too much money in the bank, you should give some away. Why? Because if you have more than you need and someone else has less, it should bring you joy to see their need met.

People are always more important than possessions. People are eternal; everything else rusts and decays. We are responsible to see that all persons have their basic needs met. He who sees his brother and sister in need and does not respond sins. We must seek equality, not just here in the United States, but throughout the world. We must accept the reality that everyone cannot live as extravagantly as we do, so we need to live less extravagantly.

No one can celebrate unless everyone can celebrate. This was the real objective of the year of jubilee. It was to be a year of celebration for everyone. Some were to celebrate receiving while others were to celebrate giving. It was to be a party.

I need to be honest with you. I still have a long way to go on these three principles. Most of the time I still think of it as my money, my house, my car, and my possessions. Only when I pause and reflect do I remember I am but a steward. Which means I need to pause and reflect more often. Most of the time I struggle to remember that people are more important than things. I want people around the world to have what I have, but I want to pretend they can have it without any sacrifice from me. But that isn't true. I need to live more simply. Most of the time I see giving to others as an obligation rather than a joy. I give money away, but I'm not always a cheerful giver.

As I was writing this chapter, a man I'd been helping called me needing to borrow money. Neal was being evicted and asked me to pay his rent. I wish I could tell you I responded with jubilee, but I didn't. I was frustrated, disappointed, angry, and resentful. It took two days for me to be thankful I was able to help Neal again. He has so little, and I have so much.

Neal was struggling because he'd recently been released from prison. He'd found a job, rented an efficiency apartment, and enrolled in college. He was trying to create a new life. Unfortunately, someone at his new job found out about his criminal history, complained to the management, and created so much animosity that Neal was fired. Neal said, "I thought I spent all those years in prison paying my debt to society, but I guess not."

His situation reminded me of the most persistent challenge to grace—justice. Many argue that believing in the salvation of all is inconsistent with God's commitment to justice. Sin and evil cannot be ignored. Sinners must be punished and the wicked destroyed. They suggest that, if Neal had committed his crimes against someone in my family, I might not be so gracious. Forgiveness and grace are utopian ideals in a harsh world where justice must trump grace.

I believe economic equality and justice are intricately connected. They can never be understood independently of each other. When justice is simply punishing evildoers, it ignores the complexities of a world in which systemic evil often goes unchallenged. What is required is a vision of justice that takes seriously the brokenness of both victim and perpetrator.

1. Thomas Merton, *No Man Is an Island* (New York: Harcourt Brace Jovanovich, 1955), p. 3. Merton offers a brilliant critique of self-absorbed love.
2. Clarence Jordan and Bill Lane Doulos, *Cotton Patch Parables of Liberation* (Scottsdale, PA: Herald Press, 1976), p. 141. This book shatters many of our middle-class assumptions about Christianity.
3. Donald Kraybill, *The Upside Down Kingdom* (Scottsdale, PA: Herald Press, 1978), p. 32. Kraybill offers a wonderful critique of how Christianity diminishes the social aspects of the gospel.
4. "Anthem Chief to Get Merit Pay of $42.5 Million," *Indianapolis Star,* April 7, 2004.
5. William Boyer, *Myth America: Democracy vs. Capitalism* (New York: Apex Press, 2003), p. 96. Boyer offers a convincing analysis of how capitalism can often undercut the principles of democracy.

6. Adam Smith, *The Wealth of Nations* (New York: Random House, 1994), p. 15.
7. Quoted in Boyer, *Myth America,* p. 18.
8. "Resurrecting the Revolutionary Heart of Judaism," *The Sun,* April 2004, p. 15.
9. John Roth, *Choosing Against War* (Intercourse, PA: Good Books, 2002), p. 74. Though an apologetic for pacifism, this book also advocates an understanding of justice that is much broader than punishing evildoers.

9

Gracious Justice

I need to stop watching Christian television. It's too painful. I usually watch until someone says something so ungracious I have to switch channels. That seldom takes more than a few minutes. Watching Christian television discourages me more often than it inspires me.

In the weeks following September 11, Christian television was especially ungracious. Some commentators condemned terrorists. Others attacked Islam. All supported swift and violent retribution. One Sunday afternoon, I caught Dr. D. James Kennedy, the pastor of the Coral Ridge Presbyterian Church and the chancellor of Knox Theological Seminary, preaching on Jesus's command to turn the other cheek.

After reading the scripture, he chronicled the events of September 11. He spoke of his horror, sorrow, and anger, all of which were appropriate responses to that heinous attack.

Then he warned his congregation there would be people such as the Quakers who would insist on seeking peace and twist the Scriptures to support their false teaching. He explained that turning the other cheek and loving your enemy didn't apply in this situation. Those commands applied only in personal relationships—with a family member, a friend, or a neighbor.

Dr. Kennedy reminded his congregation the Lord Almighty was a just God—one who did not allow iniquities to go unpunished. He announced that Osama bin Laden would soon experience God's justice at the hands of America. Islam was the enemy, and the United States was the army of the Lord. We would vanquish our enemies and avenge the deaths of the innocents. The congregation stood and cheered as the choir broke into "The Battle Hymn of the Republic." I had to switch channels.

It wasn't because I don't love my country. I was as appalled as anyone by the events of September 11. It wasn't because his sermon was so militant and violent, though I'll admit to being an adherent of the Quaker teaching called pacifism. It wasn't because he was so dismissive of Islam, a religion with many fine qualities. I switched channels because in the face of such horrible events it was so tempting to agree with him, to abandon my commitment to grace.

The events of September 11 happened while I was in the midst of writing *If Grace Is True*—my argument for the ultimate salvation of all people. Suddenly my theological speculation was put to the test. Did I believe God's grace and salvation included these men who crashed planes filled with innocent men, women, and children into buildings where they killed thousands? Did I really advocate grace and forgiveness as a legitimate and effective response?

Dr. Kennedy assured his congregation the terrorists weren't enjoying the pleasures of heaven they'd anticipated as a reward for their martyrdom. They were burning in a hell hotter than the one they ignited on the top floors of the World Trade Center. I understood how this thought could be comforting and my suggestion, that all would be redeemed and transformed, could seem a terrible injustice. Dr. Kennedy voiced the struggle of many. Can Jesus be serious about turning the other cheek or loving the enemy? Can that possibly apply to terrorists? Can anyone expect a nation, even one many claim to be Christian, to live by those words?

Perhaps Dr. Kennedy was right, that turning the other cheek is a personal act, noble and gracious, but effective only in limited situations. Having been the target of some serious bullying in the seventh grade, I've always had an elevated sense of injustice. If I see someone else struck on the cheek, I don't ask the victim to turn the other cheek. I intervene to stop the abuse. The one who strikes another should be stopped. If that violence is severe, the person should be arrested, convicted, and imprisoned. If someone commits an act of terror, I don't excuse or diminish such evil. I support efforts to protect the innocent and punish the culprits.

However, I don't accept Dr. Kennedy's neat division of grace and justice. I don't believe forgiveness is a theological idea with little practical application in a world of criminals and terrorists. I don't think justice and grace must be rivals. The prophet Micah says: "He has told you, O mortal, what is good; and what does the Lord require of you but to do justice, and to love kindness, and to walk humbly with your God?" (Micah 6:8). Micah thought you could do justice and love kindness. Jesus warned, "You tithe mint, dill, and cumin, and have neglected the weightier matters of the law: justice and mercy and faith" (Matthew 23:23). Jesus implied justice and mercy walk hand in hand. If we ever hope to live graciously in a complicated world, they must.

Complicated Justice

The events of September 11 have altered our culture in ways we're only beginning to comprehend. The most obvious change has been in our sense of invulnerability. We'd thought terrorism was something that happened elsewhere in the world. Suddenly our defenses, the most powerful and sophisticated money could buy, were worthless. Million-dollar nuclear weapons couldn't stop men armed with two-dollar box cutters. One of the common questions after September 11 was, "How could this happen to us?"

That wasn't the most difficult question. One of my friends asked, "Why did someone hate us so much they were willing to kill themselves in order to harm us?" This attack shattered our image of the United States as a benevolent and generous nation leading a grateful world into a bright future. Labeling these men as religious fanatics and terrorists eased some of our confusion, but seeing people dance in the streets of some Islamic cities enraged us. There was nearly unanimous support for President Bush's determination to bring Osama bin Laden and his henchmen to justice. Most of us quickly moved from seeking understanding to seeking revenge. I was as vulnerable to this temptation as anyone and, though a pacifist, found myself unable to object to our attack on Afghanistan. We had to do something.

Yet I was also haunted by my friend's question. Why were these young men willing to die? Mark Juergensmeyer, in his book *Terror in the Mind of God,* helped me understand the rationale behind terrorism. Juergensmeyer identifies three reasons terrorists give for attacking the United States.

First, we are perceived as the power behind many present and past oppressive governments. I wish I could deny that allegation, but I know we propped up the brutal government of the shah in Iran. We've meddled repeatedly in South and Central America. I remember Donald Rumsfeld, who branded Saddam Hussein a terrorist and tyrant, was the one who assured Hussein of American support when Iraq was fighting Iran. Our nation, which champions democracy, has given the Kingdom of Saudi Arabia, an oppressive monarchy, and Pakistan, a military dictatorship, our fullest support.

The second reason we are regarded as the enemy is because we are perceived as the promoters of a hedonist, immoral, and self-absorbed culture. Again, there is more truth in this accusation than I'd like to admit. When I remember much of the world knows us only by what they see on television and in movies, I can understand their revulsion. Though I question how well our media represent American values, what is the world to think of a nation that exports *The Jerry Springer Show?*

The third reason Juergensmeyer gives for the animosity

toward the United States is our economic power. We have so much more than we need and flaunt our affluence in a world where so many are struggling to survive. We are not seen as benevolent and generous, but as self-absorbed. I won't dispute this charge. I can understand how parents whose child has died of disease or malnutrition would find the United States, where we spend more money on pet food and supplies than we do on foreign aid, an easy target for anger.[1]

Why shouldn't people hate us if they associate our nation with oppressive power, immorality, and greed? It was no accident the hijackers targeted the Pentagon and the World Trade Center, the symbolic capitals of our power and wealth. We can call them terrorists and condemn their actions, but we cannot afford to ignore their complaints.

Juergensmeyer argues we shouldn't take this hate personally. "When the United States has been branded as an enemy in a cosmic war, it has been endowed with super-human—or perhaps subhuman—qualities, ones that have little to do with the people who actually live in America. It is the image of the country that has been despised—a reified notion of Americanism, not its people."[2]

Of course, we did take the attacks on September 11 personally. The terrorists didn't merely attack symbols of Americanism. They killed Americans. We demanded justice and attacked Afghanistan. And, in response to the first reports of innocent Afghans being killed by errant bombs, one military spokesman suggested this was a regrettable but necessary cost in the cause of freedom. In other words, those Afghan families shouldn't take it personally.

Collateral damage, whether in the cause of freedom or in an attack on the symbols of oppression and materialism, is unjust. Justice is too complicated and delicate to accomplish with hijacked jets or thousand-pound bombs. Justice is not about causes or symbols; it is about reconciling people.

Flying planes into buildings is wrong. Killing innocent people is immoral. Inappropriate acts must be punished. Yet we should never confuse punishing inappropriate acts with delivering justice. Punishment is only a recognition that there has been injury—not a means of bringing healing. When punishment simply multiplies pain and injury, it serves no legitimate purpose. Marcus Borg says, "Justice asks 'Why are there so many victims?' and then seeks to change the causes of victimization, that is, the way the system is structured. . . . Justice is about social transformation."[3]

Supporting dictators who torture their own people is unacceptable. Hoarding the resources of the world when children are dying of malnutrition is evil. Punishing terrorists while ignoring economic inequalities is like swatting flies while standing in sewage. Indeed, one of my fears in our attacks on Afghanistan and Iraq is that we've simply created one more reason for many in those countries to hate us—we killed their sons and daughters, their brothers and sisters. One Osama bin Laden is replaced with a hundred others.

I experienced this same dilemma when I sat through the

trial of a man accused of molesting a teenage boy. In her closing remarks, the prosecutor argued that, though this man had been molested himself as a teenager, the jury shouldn't consider his past. She also claimed child molesters couldn't change and the only way to assure the public safety was to imprison him for a long time. I couldn't help wondering what we were to think of this man's victim—was he doomed to molest someone else? Would the public be safer if we imprisoned him as well? Punishment is not justice. Justice is creating a world where both victim and perpetrator are healed and transformed, where reconciliation rather than retribution is the goal.

Justice is complicated because it must address both inappropriate actions and the situations that create and motivate negative behavior. Terrorists and child molesters must be punished or restrained, but far more important are efforts to break the cycle of systemic injustice. When punishment is socially sanctioned revenge, we do nothing to make the world a more gracious place. This is why we can do justice only if we love kindness and walk humbly with God.

Costly Grace

When I speak of the salvation of all people, I'm often accused of not taking sin and evil seriously. One critic said, "Isn't that nice? Hitler and Stalin are in heaven. How we live doesn't matter because God will forgive us in the end. No wonder people like your understanding of grace—you make life easy."

I suppose if I thought how we live didn't matter, this would make some of life's quandaries easier. I also suspect it would make life miserable. In my experience, how we live is important to us and to others. Being self-absorbed is counterproductive. We were created for relationship, and living in alienation never satisfies. Sin and evil are serious concerns not because we'll be damned for eternity, but because they make us miserable right now.

Believing in the salvation of all people eased my anxieties and ended my obsession with my ultimate destiny, but it also increased my concern for others. Knowing God loved me unconditionally was comforting, but loving others with this same grace wasn't easy. Living graciously was more difficult than the doctrine-believing, rule-keeping religion of my childhood. It was especially challenging, since I no longer had the option of identifying someone as evil or lost, beyond God's reach and my concern.

Dr. Kennedy argued Jesus didn't expect us to turn the other cheek to terrorists. He may be right. We should take reasonable, balanced precautions to prevent another slap on the cheek. But I would dispute Kennedy's claim that Jesus's words were limited to personal interactions and unrealistic in responding to societal issues. Ironically, Jesus's words were directed at those with the complaints of the terrorists—those who found themselves the victims of systemic injustice. Jesus would probably be more sympathetic toward the anger of terrorists than the arrogant, self-righteousness of the elite.

Jesus said, "Do not resist an evildoer. But if anyone strikes you on one cheek, turn the other also; and if anyone wants to sue you and take your coat, give them your cloak as well; and if anyone forces you to go one mile, go also the second mile" (Matthew 5:39–41). What Jesus was describing, and what modern readers often miss, is not personal attacks, but the behavior of an oppressive system. The person most likely to strike a Jew on the cheek or demand he carry his pack a mile was a Roman soldier. The most common reason someone took a poor person's coat, the proverbial shirt off his back, was in a legal suit or through taxation. Jesus was telling his disciples how to respond to an oppressive system.

Jesus is suggesting something far more radical than forgiving personal slights from friends and family. He is inviting his followers to a costly grace—one that responds to injustice with generosity and goodness. A Roman soldier demands you carry his pack for a mile, which was within his rights, and you offer to carry it an additional mile. A tax collector demands your coat and you give him your shirt as well. A soldier strikes you on one cheek and you offer the other.

Dr. Kennedy suggested Jesus's words aren't applicable to the events of September 11. I disagree, but I think Jesus was even more concerned about the events of September 10, when the terrorists made the decision to attack. He was challenging how the poor and oppressed respond to political and economic oppression, whether from the Roman Empire or the United States of America. He was inviting those who were considering a violent uprising or flying airplanes into buildings to a more costly grace. Were they willing to transform evil by absorbing and redeeming pain and injury? Were they willing to challenge oppressive power by demonstrating its inability to destroy or twist their humanity?

Jesus wasn't naive. He knew what evil could do. Rome would often line the roads of Palestine with crosses. Jesus must have walked between those crosses many times on his way to Jerusalem. The anger and hatred behind the September 11 attack wouldn't have surprised him. He knew years of desperation make it difficult for some to choose grace instead of violence. Yet Jesus commanded his disciples to carry crosses rather than swords.

Jesus not only taught this; he lived it. In those hours before his death, he was spit upon, slapped, whipped, mocked, and bloodied. Yet Jesus prayed for the forgiveness of those who did these things. When he rose from the dead, he didn't seek out those who had killed him and demand his pound of flesh. He commanded his disciples to spread the kingdom of God—this kingdom of grace—throughout the world. There seems only one fair conclusion—Jesus was serious about his command to turn the other cheek and love our enemies. He also knew how costly grace could be.

Of course, as I pointed out in the previous chapter, it wasn't from only the poor and oppressed that Jesus expected costly grace. Though there are no excuses for what happened on September 11, there is also no excuse for the apathy of the rich and powerful. Jesus said, "From everyone to whom much has been given, much will be required; and from the one to whom much has been entrusted, even more will be demanded" (Luke 12:48).

Dietrich Bonhoeffer, in his classic *The Cost of Discipleship,* writes: "Cheap grace is the preaching of forgiveness without requiring repentance, baptism without church discipline, communion without confession, absolution without personal confession. Cheap grace is grace without discipleship, grace without a cross, grace without Jesus Christ, living and incarnate."[4]

Cheap grace also justifies severe economic inequality while condemning terrorist activity, forgives greed and gluttony while imprisoning petty thieves, blesses bombs and sanctifies war without asking what makes bombs and war necessary. Cheap grace is grace for the rich and swift punishment for the poor, grace without personal sacrifice, grace without Jesus's teachings, living and incarnate.

Costly grace means challenging injustice, either personal or systemic, and accepting responsibility for our contributions to injustice. The issue is not who is most to blame—who is right and who is wrong—but how we find a way to live in equality and peace. We all begin by looking inward. How am I making the world a less gracious place?

We all are guilty of self-absorption. We begin the transformation of the world by transforming ourselves. We do this gently and, in the process of removing the splinter from our eye, discover why taking the splinter from the eye of our enemy is such delicate work. We are commanded to fight injustice passionately, but gently, rejecting violence and acknowledging the pain of our enemy. Thomas Merton says, "Ideally speaking, nonviolent action is supposed to be conducted in such a way that both sides come to see the injustice as a disadvantage and a dishonor to both, and they then agree to work together to remedy things."[5]

Costly grace asks the poor and oppressed to turn the other cheek, to surrender both shirt and coat, to walk the second mile. Costly grace also asks the rich and powerful to acknowledge their contribution to systemic injustice—to cease benefiting from or ignoring the misery of others. Both rich and poor must swallow their pride.

This admission is difficult for those who are oppressed. The desire to lash back is often overwhelming, resulting in inner-city riots and suicide bombers. Even more difficult is the admission of injustice by those in power. The temptation to justify a system of personal comfort is beguiling. During the height of the civil rights movement, Dr. Martin Luther King Jr. wrote of slavery what could be said of any systemic injustice:

> Slavery in America was perpetuated not merely by human badness but also by human blindness. The casual basis for the system of slavery must to large extent be traced back to the economic factor. Men convinced themselves that a system which was so economically profitable must be morally justifiable. They formulated elaborate theories of racial superiority. Their rationalizations clothed obvious wrongs in the beautiful garments of righteousness. This tragic attempt to give moral sanction to an economically profitable system gave birth to the doctrine of white supremacy. Religion and the Bible were cited to crystallize the status quo. Science was commandeered to prove the biological inferiority of the Negro. Even philosophical logic was manipulated to give intellectual credence to a system of slavery. [6]

Costly grace demands those who've benefited from economic and political injustice cease their efforts to rationalize injustice. We have no excuse. In a world where famine and disease are visible on the nightly news, where statisticians track how many die unnecessarily each day, and where the resources are available to care for every person, ethical blindness is curable. In order to create a gracious world, we must open our eyes and acknowledge our responsibility.

Cheap grace is what we give to ourselves—forgiveness and acceptance without repentance and change. Costly grace comes in committing ourselves to paying the price for seeing every life blessed. Unfortunately, we normally expend our energies in protecting the status quo. President Bush, in the days after September 11, suggested we were fighting to defend our way of life. But what if our way of life is unjust and oppressive toward much of the world?

When we fail to acknowledge our complicity in the injustice in the world, we often replace real justice—economic and political equality—with retribution. What we seek is not to rectify injustice, but to defend our inordinate piece of the pie. The answer is "homeland security" rather than global equality. We seek an eye for an eye and a tooth for a tooth from people blinded by rage with no food to chew. Unfortunately, when we attack the poor, we seldom do justice. Ungracious justice is merciless, justifying the ugly and violating the principles we pretend to value.

Ungracious Justice

Many of the Sunday school stories of my childhood were troubling—God commanding the killing of innocents in Canaan, God striking down Uzzah, God killing the child of David and Bathsheba as punishment, and God killing all of Job's children to win a debate with Satan. I wanted to believe that "God is patient with [us], not wanting any to perish, but all to come to repentance" (2 Peter 3:9). But story after story suggested God was not only impatient—God was also unjust.

Eventually, I decided the Bible does what human beings have always done—we attribute to God actions and attitudes we want to defend. We kill innocent men, women, and children and claim the mandate of God. This happened in Canaan thousands of years ago and happens in New York City and Afghanistan today. We blame misfortune on unfaithfulness, whether with Uzzah or with a homosexual with HIV. We interpret disaster as a punishment from God and excuse collateral damage as acceptable in a noble cause. So what if God killed all the firstborn in Egypt? He made his point to Pharaoh. So what if we kill thousands of Iraqis? We brought them freedom.

I agree with Dr. Kennedy—God is just. The problem is we keep justifying our actions rather than making our actions just. We wrap wrath, revenge, and retribution in the robes of justice and lay the bloody victims on the altars of our religions. No biblical story makes this more obvious than the rape of Dinah in Genesis 34.

If you're unfamiliar with this story—one that, fortunately, we don't teach our children in Sunday school—don't be too concerned. It is not one of humanity's brightest moments. In the story, Jacob and his family have settled outside the city of Shechem, bought some land, and erected an altar. Dinah, Jacob's daughter, begins to befriend the women of Shechem and meets one of the princes of that city—the son of Hamor, the king of Shechem. (I should acknowledge that many scholars believe this story is more of a parable about the dangers of intermarriage than a historic event, but the lessons about injustice remain.)

Dinah and the son of Hamor have sex. The Bible says this was rape, but also admits the boy and girl were lovers. Jacob and his sons were outraged by this relationship, although they were less concerned about Dinah and more interested in defending their honor. The son of Hamor had taken what belonged to them—Dinah.

When Hamor comes to Jacob to ask him to allow his son and Dinah to marry, the sons of Jacob demand Hamor and the men of Shechem be circumcised. Unfortunately, this requirement was not motivated by a desire to be unified in custom and religion with the Shechemites, but was part of a plot to avenge this affront. When the men of Shechem were incapacitated by their circumcisions, the sons of Jacob killed every man in Shechem and plundered the city. "All their wealth, all their little ones and their wives, all that was in their houses, they captured and made their prey" (Genesis 34:29). The only redeeming aspect of this story was that the sons of Jacob never claimed they were acting on God's behalf.

This is a story about injustice justified. It reminds us how often defending our honor is the underlying motive behind our causes and crusades. How dare they do such a thing to us? We aren't seeking justice, but defending our proper place in the pecking order. We aren't really concerned about the people in a conflict, but in coming out on top. We aren't seeking a solution, but conquest. When the United States declares war on terrorism, are we doing justice or reasserting our dominance? Was September 11 an excuse for us to throw our weight around?

Dinah's situation was clearly an excuse for Jacob and his sons to exert power. There is no indication Jacob or his sons ever considered Dinah's wishes. They called her lovemaking with the son of Hamor a defilement—a rape. They also called their murder of every man in Shechem—including all those who'd never touched Dinah—justice. A clear sign of injustice is the objectifying of people. When causes or symbols become more important than love and relationship, we can justify anything—killing the man our sister loves, flying planes into buildings, or bombing villages.

Jacob and his sons not only objectified people; they betrayed their own religious values. They used circumcision—a symbol of cultural and religious unity and faithfulness—as a means to accomplish their revenge. In so doing, they called into question their commitment to what they said mattered. Injustice loves to wrap itself in religious language and symbols, but has no respect for its values. Killing yourself and innocents by flying a plane into a building doesn't honor Allah. It violates the clear admonitions against suicide and murder. Excusing ourselves from having to turn the other cheek or care for the poor isn't obeying Jesus. Too often we use the language of justice to justify our greed.

The sons of Jacob committed more than murder; they were thieves. The fact that they plundered Shechem calls into question their motives. Was it justice or economic gain that inspired their attack? Injustice always lines its pockets. In revolution after revolution, those who overthrow oppressive governments often become oppressive themselves. We can't resist the spoils of victory. That American oil companies will dominate in the new Iraq makes our claims of fighting for freedom ring hollow. That we have killed far more Afghans and Iraqis than the number of Americans killed on September 11 undercuts even the requirement for retribution—it must be proportional.

The sons of Jacob didn't kill only the son of Hamor—the man they alleged had raped Dinah—they killed everyone in Shechem. This is the final sign of injustice. Revenge isn't even satisfied with evening the score—it seeks to elimi-

nate the opponent from the game. It does this because it recognizes, at some level, its own futility. Unless we destroy our
enemy, we know our enemy will have even more reason to
hate and harm us. This may explain why Joshua commanded the Israelites not only to kill all the males in the
cities they conquered, but the women and children as well.
The children of the one I destroy will one day seek revenge.

It was in response to this issue of proportion that Judaism adopted a code of retribution. Moses said, "If anyone
injures his neighbor, whatever he has done must be done to
him: fracture for fracture, eye for eye, tooth for tooth. As he
has injured the other, so he is to be injured" (Leviticus
24:19–20). Revenge was domesticated. Justice stood blindfolded, measuring out retribution on carefully calibrated
scales, inflicting pain equal only to what one caused.

This concept of justice, though certainly an improve-
ment over the behavior of the sons of Jacob, still objectified
people. The Hebrew Scriptures dealt with situations like
that of Dinah. "If a man meets a virgin who is not engaged,
and seizes her and lies with her, and they are caught in the
act, the man who lay with her shall give fifty shekels of silver to the young woman's father, and she shall become his
wife" (Deuteronomy 22:28–29). Sins were paid for in either
blood or money. Evening the scales, rather than reconciliation, was the goal.

Jesus didn't share this understanding of justice. He proclaimed, "You have heard that it was said, 'An eye for an
eye, and tooth for a tooth.' But I say to you, Do not resist an

evildoer. If someone strikes you on the right cheek, turn to him the other also" (Matthew 5:38–39). "You have heard that it was said, 'You shall love your neighbor and hate your enemy.' But I say to you, Love your enemies and pray for those who persecute you" (Matthew 5:43–44).

These are the words of Jesus. We don't have to like them. We don't have to obey them. But if we are serious about being his disciples, we can't ignore them. We have to understand why Jesus would command such nonsense.

Dr. Kennedy believed Quakers were fools to think turning the other cheek and loving the enemy could apply in a post–September 11 world. I wonder if the fools are those who can't see that thousands of years of an eye for eye, a tooth for a tooth, an attack for an attack, a war for a war, a holocaust for a holocaust have utterly failed to eliminate the pain of the world. We are fools when we look back over our bloody history and refuse to try something different—even something as odd as turning the other cheek.

Reconciling Justice

When I first began considering the possibility that God would save every person, I decided to read the Bible from cover to cover looking for any passages supporting such an idea. I found many universalist themes throughout Scripture. Paul, in proclaiming the supremacy of Christ, says, "For in him [Jesus] all the fullness of God was pleased to dwell, and through him God was pleased to reconcile to himself all things, whether on earth or in heaven, by making peace through the blood of his cross" (Colossians 1:19–20). Though I no longer hold this view of incarnation or atonement, I still find the desire of God to reconcile all things radical theology.

The problem with dualistic theologies is that God's desire is to separate the wheat from the chaff, the sheep from the goats, the saved from the damned. In this theological framework, justice separates and punishes rather than reconciles and restores. If some people will never be healed and the wicked eternally punished, if God's grace will be insufficient to save many, we too can be satisfied with balancing the scales.

Believing every person will be saved is much more than theological speculation. It is a social commitment. If God desires to reconcile all people to one another, we are to be about the business of reconciliation now. Elsewhere, Paul writes, "In Christ, God was reconciling the world to himself, not counting their trespasses against them, and entrusting the message of reconciliation to us" (2 Corinthians 5:19). Justice, in a theology of grace, is committed to reconciliation.

Proportional justice will never bring the healing we seek. It can only multiply the pain. Jesus did not call us to retaliation, but to gracious justice, seeking to reconcile victim and perpetrator. Why? Because only reconciliation has the power to end pain and transform human behavior. Jesus did not ask us to weigh our pains on carefully calibrated scales. He did not encourage us to respond to pain with equal pain. He did not command us to return evil for evil. Jesus invited us to take up a cross—to join him in forgiving those who do evil and absorbing the pain of the world.

Absorbing pain is what turning the other cheek and loving your enemy require. We don't ignore our pain, but we refuse to cause additional suffering. For both victim and perpetrator this is costly. The perpetrator must accept punishment and repentance as the necessary cost of reconciliation. The victim must learn grace and forgiveness are the first steps to healing.

Our present system does a very poor job of reconciliation. Over the past ten years I've worked with a family broken by the sexual abuse of the stepdaughter by the stepfather. When the stepfather was arrested, he and I agreed that he should do nothing to increase the pain he'd caused his step-daughter.

This meant taking complete responsibility for his crime, keeping his stepdaughter from having to testify, accepting a harsh plea bargain, and being sentenced to fifteen years in prison—the sentence his stepdaughter requested from the judge. This was a difficult decision when his lawyer and his fellow prisoners were encouraging him to use every strategy to escape punishment. This was especially challenging to a man whose self-absorption had led to his crime. Going to prison took grace and courage.

During his first few years in prison, he lost contact with his family. He sent letters expressing his continued remorse, accepting his responsibility, and asking for forgiveness and reconciliation. His letters went unanswered. This was painful for him, but he was not the only one in pain.

His stepdaughter had also been traumatized. Her family, having lost their chief breadwinner, was financially devastated. Her stepbrothers, who'd lost their father to prison, were resentful. The stigma of others knowing of her molestation was embarrassing. Yet on her eighteenth birthday, she chose to visit her stepfather. She did this aware she was violating the restraining order the court had placed on them. Going to see her stepfather in prison took grace and courage.

It was a tearful meeting, but after two hours of confession and discussion, their reconciliation began. Several years later, she joined in an effort to have her stepfather's sentence modified. She no longer needed him to be sitting in prison. Unfortunately, a justice system based on retribution is incapable of recognizing that reconciliation, not punishment, should be its goal. Her plea went unheard.

This stepfather and stepdaughter absorbed the pain and allowed reconciliation to occur. They each turned the other cheek, walked the second mile, gave cloak as well as shirt. Those examples were Jesus's way of teaching the most effective way of transforming hostile human relationships—we create the space for the other person to see our common humanity. To love kindness is to be committed to helping everyone—even our enemies—to see our kinship.

The goal is not to shame the ones causing pain, though this often happens, but to transform them. Paul says, "No, 'if your enemies are hungry, feed them; if they are thirsty, give them something to drink; for by doing this you heap burning coals on their heads'" (Romans 12:20). I wish Paul meant those coals to be purifying rather than punitive. Thomas Merton said, "Thomas à Becket, in Eliot's play *Murder in the Cathedral,* debated with himself, fearing that he might be seeking martyrdom merely in order to demonstrate his own righteousness and the King's injustice: 'This is the greatest treason, to do the right thing for the wrong reason.'"[7]

Our task is not to humiliate the ones who cause pain and injustice, but to help them recognize that we are human beings like them, with equal value. We are also calling them away from division and toward relationship. Turning the other cheek as an act of defiance avails nothing. Walking the second mile because we love our enemies changes minds and hearts.

Imagine for a moment a first-century Jew being forced to carry a Roman soldier's pack. The soldier has all the power. He commands and humiliates the Jew. Power triumphs. Imagine that Jew choosing to carry the pack a second mile. The entire relationship changes. The peasant commands himself and brings dignity to his relationship with the soldier. Grace trumps power.

Dr. Kennedy might object that once again we're speaking of personal relationships—a stepfather and stepdaughter, one soldier abusing one peasant. How can such an approach apply to the enmity between the United States and terrorists? How do we absorb the pain of thousands?

John Roth, in his book *Choosing Against War,* reminds us of a recent attempt. When apartheid collapsed in South Africa in 1994, many predicted a bloodbath as poor blacks took revenge on an oppressive white minority who had committed horrible crimes. This didn't happen. Much of the credit for this gracious transition must go to Nelson Mandela, a victim of injustice and a champion of reconciliation, who established the Truth and Reconciliation Commission. The goal of this commission was not simply to punish, but to reconcile blacks and whites.

Roth tells of an elderly woman whose son had been taken by white police officers, shot, and his body set on fire as the men celebrated around the fire. Eight years later, these same men took her husband, tied him to a pile of wood, doused him with gasoline, and set him afire. In 1994, she finally faced the leader of this group, Mr. Van de Broek, as the court prepared to pass sentence.

Roth writes:

Those involved had confessed their guilt, and the Commission turned to the woman for a final statement regarding her desire for an appropriate punishment.

"I want three things," the woman said calmly. "I want Mr. Van de Broek to take me to the place where they burned my husband's body. I would like to gather up the dust and give him a decent burial.

"Second, Mr. Van de Broek took all my family away from me, and I still have a lot to give. Twice a month, I would like him to come to the ghetto and spend the day with me so I can be a mother to him.

"Third, I would like Mr. Van de Broek to know he is forgiven by God and that I forgive him, too. And, I would like someone to come and lead me by the hand to where Mr. Van de Broek is so that I can embrace him and he can know my forgiveness is real."[8]

I won't pretend this woman's words and actions are common, but they are authentically Christian. I won't imply that every meeting of the Truth and Reconciliation Commission was as exemplary, but neither will I accept the assertion that retributive, proportional justice is the only practical system. Democratic governments can choose to move beyond revenge and retribution.

What would have happened if the United States had chosen to absorb the pain of September 11? How would such graciousness have changed the future? How would it have altered the attitude of many toward our country? How would fanatics recruit additional terrorists to attack a nation that forgave its enemies? I understand how radical this suggestion seems, but I question whether anything we have done has made the world a safer and more gracious place. Violence is incapable of redeeming our world.

Mahatma Gandhi thought *ahimsa*—literally translated "nonkilling"—to be the only hope for social transformation. He argued that those who take up weapons and respond violently misunderstand their humanity and the religious obligation to suffer for others. He wrote:

> Non-violence is a perfect state. It is a goal towards which all mankind moves naturally, though unconsciously. . . . In our present state, we are partly men and partly beasts, and in our ignorance and even arrogance say that we truly fulfill the purpose of our species, when we deliver blow for blow and develop the measure of anger required for the purpose. We pretend to believe that retaliation is the Law of our Being, whereas in every scripture we

IF GOD IS LOVE

find that retaliation is nowhere obligatory but only permissible. It is restraint that is obligatory. Retaliation is indulgence, requiring elaborate regulating. Restraint is the Law of our Being. For, highest perfection is unattainable without highest restraint. Suffering is thus the badge of the human tribe.[9]

For the Christian, suffering is not to be feared. The resurrection of Jesus and his proclamation of eternal life is the reason we can begin to live graciously right now. We don't have to waste our energies on defending ourselves, measuring pain for pain, and delivering blow for blow. Convinced life is eternal, we are freed to risk doing that which, though uncommon, is the highest and noblest—offering forgiveness to even our enemies.

For those who believe in the salvation of all, this obligation is even more compelling. Justice is no longer about waiting for the Last Judgment, when God will separate the sheep from the goats. Justice happens when God's will is done on earth as it is in heaven, when we forgive as God has forgiven us, when we love as God loves, when enemies are reconciled, when brothers and sisters embrace.

When politics, economics, and systems of justice become gracious, the world will begin to change—a kingdom of goodness and grace will arise. For two thousand years, Christians have been waiting for Jesus to return and initiate this kingdom. We've waited too long. There is no good reason for another generation to live in an ungracious world.

1. Mark Juergensmeyer, *Terror in the Mind of God* (Berkeley and Los Angeles: University of California Press, 2000), pp. 178–82. Juergensmeyer, who wrote his book shortly before September 11, proved prophetic in many ways. His examination of terrorist tendencies in all the great religions is frightening reading.

2. Juergensmeyer, *Terror,* p. 182.

3. Marcus Borg, *The Heart of Christianity* (San Francisco: HarperSanFrancisco, 2003), p. 201. Borg offers many practical ideas for practicing both compassion and justice.

4. Dietrich Bonhoeffer, *The Cost of Discipleship* (New York: Macmillan, 1949), p. 47. Though Bonhoeffer discusses grace in religious terms, his suggestion that grace without responsibility is cheap applies to any discussion of justice.

5. Thomas Merton, *Faith and Violence* (Notre Dame, IN: University of Notre Dame Press, 1968), p. 37. Merton wrote these essays as he struggled with the conflict in Vietnam. Unfortunately, they continue to be relevant.

6. Martin Luther King Jr., *Strength to Love* (Philadelphia, PA: Fortress Press, 1963), p. 44. This collection of sermons and essays time and again connects the imperative to resist evil and injustice with the call to grace and forgiveness.

7. Merton, *Faith and Violence,* p. 19.

8. John Roth, *Choosing Against War* (Intercourse, PA: Good Books, 2002), p. 63. Roth offers a compelling argument against war and many practical suggestions for institutionalizing reconciliation rather than revenge.

9. Mahatma Gandhi, *The Law of Love* (Bombay: Bharatiya, Vidya Bhavan, 1946), p. 21.

10

A Gracious World

❦

The preachers of my childhood loved the book of Revelation, with its prophecies of gloom and doom. They would often remind us Jesus could return in the twinkling of an eye, when least expected. They were quick to see an earthquake in China, a war in the Middle East, and every action by the Vatican or the United Nations as a sure sign of the end. They decried the growing wickedness of the world and pled with us to come to the altar before it was too late. They warned us that, when Christ came for the Church, we didn't want to be left behind.

Such appeals were frightening to me. I recall lying in bed at night, after I'd done something wrong, worried I might awake the next morning to find my family gone. As a teenager, I prayed Jesus wouldn't come back until I'd had sex. When I confessed this to my youth pastor, he assured me heaven would be much better than sex. Having nothing to compare heaven with, I kept praying. In college, we all read Hal Lindsey's *The Late Great Planet Earth,* which carefully dissected the book of Revelation, identifying grasshoppers as helicopters, the Beast as the European Common Market, and the Antichrist as a liberal political leader.

Jesus may have said no one knew the hour or day of his return, but we knew exactly how the end would happen. The Church would be raptured (taken up into heaven), although we argued passionately about whether this would occur before, during, or at the end of the tribulation. There would be seven years of unbridled evil followed by the battle of Armageddon, in which Christ and his army would destroy the Russians, Chinese, Arabs, and anyone else who wasn't Christian. The Second Coming would be violent and Jesus would no longer be meek and mild. "From his mouth comes a sharp sword with which to strike down the nations, and he will rule them with a rod of iron: he will tread the wine press of the fury of the wrath of God the Almighty" (Revelation 19:15).

It would be years before I learned the Apocalypse of John was one of many political critiques written by the early Church, that there is strong evidence its author was writing in response to persecution by the Roman Empire, and that the Antichrist was probably the emperor Nero. I discovered its inclusion in the biblical canon was often challenged and that many thought it should be read as an allegory rather than as prophecy. I was relieved to find not everyone thought the reign of God would come in a cataclysmic finale. But even before I learned all of this, I didn't understand how the Jesus of the Second Coming could be so unlike the Jesus of the first.

Reading other apocalyptic passages in the Bible didn't help matters. The Gospels had Jesus predicting events like those in Revelation. He promised he would come in the clouds with great power and glory, sending his angels to gather his elect from the ends of the earth. Unfortunately, the Gospels also had Jesus saying, "Truly, I tell you, this generation will not pass away until all these things have taken place" (Mark 13:30). When I asked about this error, I was offered a variety of explanations, all of which assumed Jesus couldn't have meant what he said.

What became clear was that many in the early Church expected Jesus to return quickly, within their lifetime. They envisioned this return as quite different from his first appearance. This time Jesus wouldn't end up on a cross. He'd sit on a throne. He would judge the nations, cast his enemies into hell, and establish the kingdom of God. Jesus would wipe away every tear—death, mourning, crying and pain would be no more.

Those were powerful and compelling images, especially when we remember how horribly the early Church was being persecuted. It's understandable why many would hope for Christ's return and why this Second Coming emphasized wrath rather than grace. Those slaughtered for their faithfulness were pictured crying out, "Sovereign Lord, holy and true, how long will it be before you judge and avenge our blood on the inhabitants of the earth?" (Revelation 6:10).

For whatever reason, God has not elected to avenge their suffering. Jesus has not returned as a political or military leader to set things right. Though Christian leaders throughout history have predicted the hour or the day of Christ's return, they've all been wrong. Those hoping for wrath continue to wait. They also continue to warn and threaten.

In 1988, Edgar Whisenant mailed a self-published book entitled *88 Reasons the Rapture Could Be in 1988* to nearly every pastor in the United States. He convinced thousands of Christians to stay home from work during the second week of September in order to be raptured as a family. When the date came and passed, he never mailed a retraction or an apology. He simply revised his prediction to 1989 and kept waiting.

Edgar Whisenant was not the first to be disappointed when a divinely anointed military and political leader failed to appear. He's in good company. John the Baptist also told the religious folk of his day the end was near. He promised the arrival of the Messiah they'd been waiting for—one who'd "clear his threshing floor and gather the wheat into his granary; but the chaff he will burn with unquenchable fire" (Luke 3:17). He didn't predict a date, but he identified a person. The Messiah was Jesus.

Unfortunately, Jesus was not what John the Baptist had hoped for or expected. He didn't fit the image most Jews had of the Messiah. Jesus was more critical of his own religion than he was of the Roman occupation. He was more interested in healing people than attacking his enemies. His chief act of rebellion was to clear the Temple. He was a disappointment and eventually an embarrassment. He refused to be who they wanted him to be.

A Disappointing Messiah

Years ago, I saw the musical *Jesus Christ Superstar*. It begins with Judas singing, "Listen, Jesus, I don't like what I see. All I ask is that you listen to me. And remember, I've been your right-hand man all along. You have set them all on fire. They think they've found the new Messiah. And they'll hurt you when they find they're wrong." His warning may explain what happened in the days between Palm Sunday, when Jesus was welcomed with waving branches, and Good Friday, when Jesus was met with waving fists. Judas wasn't the only one having second thoughts about Jesus; nearly everyone was.

The Jews had been waiting hundreds of years for the Messiah. He was to be the one anointed by God to bring good news, to free the captives, to heal the blind, and to proclaim the year of God's favor. He was to usher in the kingdom of God. Isaiah was full of prophecies about the Messiah—one who would save Israel and conquer its enemies. "He will faithfully bring forth justice. He will not grow faint or be crushed until he had established justice in the earth" (Isaiah 42:3–4). The "he" was the Messiah.

Since the Messiah was to bring justice, it should be no surprise that, when the Jews were experiencing injustice, they would yearn for his coming. Jesus was born in such a time. The Romans controlled Judea with a cruel fist. The Jews were ready for a Messiah. Any charismatic leader was likely to be anointed.

When Jesus asked his disciples who they thought he was, Peter answered, "You are the Messiah" (Mark 8:29). This was a reasonable response. Jesus was gathering a considerable following. He was doing miracles. He was talking of the kingdom of God. He was using the language of Isaiah.

According to the Gospels, Jesus accepted this title. He said he was the one they'd been waiting for. He also warned them not to tell anyone—an odd command from someone preparing to lead a political and military campaign. Commentators suggest this warning indicated Jesus wasn't ready to take his throne. There is another possibility. Perhaps Jesus never intended to take a throne. He knew his understanding of the Messiah and that of his contemporaries were not the same.

Most Jews expected the Messiah to be a military leader, a new King David, who would lead a human army and establish an earthly kingdom. Others thought he would also be a religious leader and cleanse Judaism, destroying those Jews who'd made compromises with the Greeks and Romans. All believed the Messiah would separate the wheat from the chaff.

We begin to see why Judas, in *Jesus Christ Superstar,* had his fears about Jesus's claiming to be the Messiah. For those who wanted a general, talk of turning the other cheek, of loving your enemy, and of walking the second mile was treason. For those expecting a religious leader to cleanse Judaism, eating with sinners and tax collectors was blasphemy. For those expecting the Messiah to carry a bloody sword, a cross was unimaginable. What would happen when he disappointed them?

And they were disappointed. John the Baptist, the first to call Jesus the Messiah, had grave doubts. He sent two of his disciples to ask Jesus, "Are you the one who is to come, or are we to wait for another?" Jesus replied, "Go and tell John what you have seen and heard: the blind receive their sight, the lame walk, the lepers are cleansed, the deaf hear, the dead are raised, the poor have good news brought to them" (Luke 7:20–22).

The Gospels don't tell us what John thought of this reply. Jesus didn't say, "I'm the one." Instead, he suggested by his answer that what he was doing, though not what John expected, was the work of the Messiah. Apparently, the kingdom Jesus believed in was considerably different from the one the Jews anticipated. What the Jews were waiting for wasn't what they were going to get.

Jesus didn't plan to lead an army, or become the high priest, or even judge the nations. His plan was simple—to heal, to bring life, to proclaim good news, to love those around him. This was the kingdom of God. It wasn't something you waited for or went searching after. It was something you either believed in or doubted. Once you believed in it, you saw it everywhere.

One day, some Pharisees asked Jesus, point blank, when the kingdom of God would come. Jesus replied, "The kingdom of God is not coming with things that can be observed; nor will they say, 'Look, here it is!' or 'There it is!' For, in fact, the kingdom of God is among you" (Luke 17:20–21). The Gospel of Thomas, a collection of sayings by Jesus not included in our New Testament, has a similar quote. Jesus's disciples ask him, "When will the Kingdom come?" Jesus replies, "It will not come by watching for it. They will not say, 'Look, it is here!' or 'Look, it is there!' Rather, the Kingdom of the Father is spread out upon the earth, but people do not see it" (113).[1]

The answer to the problems of life was not in some divine warrior descending from heaven to smite the evildoers. It was not in lifting some human leader to prominence and expecting him to right every injustice. It was in accepting the responsibility we each have to allow the kingdom of God to reign in our hearts. No wonder Jesus was crucified. He refused to be who we wanted him to be. He insisted we should stop looking to heaven and start looking within ourselves. We should stop waiting.

Why We Can't Wait

When I was growing up, I experienced an odd contradiction. On one hand, we were encouraged to save souls. Since no one knew the hour or day of their own death or of Christ's return, there was great urgency in telling others about Christ and getting them to make a confession of faith.

On the other hand, we were often discouraged from getting involved in societal issues. Since the world was tainted by evil and doomed to destruction, there was no obligation to invest ourselves in redeeming human institutions. Peace, unity, and even justice were pipe dreams until Jesus returned. Our task was to be ready and waiting.

When I became convinced God would save every person I realized there was no reason to wait. There were no lost souls or lost causes. I needed to get out of the pew and into the world. The religious were to be agents of transformation rather than allies of the status quo. I also recognized how frightening this message can be to those who've been praying for deliverance and how challenging it can be to those who find their circumstances comfortable. Telling people to stop waiting and start changing can be dangerous.

In *Why We Can't Wait,* Dr. Martin Luther King Jr. responded to those who asked him to be patient, that

Christianity would eventually win equal rights for African Americans. He wrote,

> Such an attitude stems from a tragic misconception of time, from the strangely irrational notion that there is something in the very flow of time that will inevitably cure all ills. Actually, time itself is neutral; it can be used either destructively or constructively. More and more I feel that people of ill will have used time much more effectively than have people of good will. We will have to repent in this generation not merely for hateful words and actions of the bad people but for the appalling silence of the good people. Human progress never rolls in on the wheels of inevitability; it comes through the tireless efforts of men willing to be coworkers with God, and without this hard work, time itself becomes an ally of the forces of social stagnation.[2]

The problem with waiting is that nothing really changes. The problem with change is that it requires our involvement. King paid with his life for his insistence that justice and freedom couldn't wait. The cost of such courage is a deterrent to action, but far more often we wait because we hope someone, perhaps God, will do the dirty and difficult work of transforming our world.

This is an age-old malaise. The oldest Hebrew Scriptures challenge this human tendency. God says, "Now what

I am commanding you today is not too difficult for you or beyond your reach. It is not up in heaven, so that you have to ask, 'Who will ascend into heaven to get it and proclaim it to us so we may obey it?' Nor is it beyond the sea, so that you have to ask, 'Who will cross the sea to get it and proclaim it to us so we may obey it?' No, the word is very near you; it is in your mouth and in your heart so you may obey it" (Deuteronomy 30:11–14, NIV). We need to stop waiting for someone to ascend to or descend from heaven.

Unfortunately, our inclination is to look everywhere but within ourselves. In 1964, Kitty Genovese was murdered on a street in New York City. Thirty-eight people heard or saw her being attacked and not a single person did anything. Many couldn't understand how such a terrible thing could happen.

A. M. Rosenthall interviewed the thirty-eight witnesses. He discovered two primary excuses for their inactivity. Many said they thought it was an issue for the police and they didn't want to get involved. When they were asked why they didn't call the police, they replied that they thought someone else would. None of them accepted their responsibility to intervene. Why? Rosenthall doesn't say, but I would suggest what incapacitated them was fear.

Isn't this always what keeps the kingdom of God from becoming a reality? We see an injustice and we complain to heaven. Why doesn't God intervene? We see a problem and we look for someone to solve it. Why doesn't the government do something? We never admit that what keeps us from acting is our lack of courage. What if I act and I too become a victim of evil? What if I speak up and I too become a target? What if I reach out and others reject me? What if I act and I fail? And, most frightening, what if the change must begin within me?

The wheat and chaff need to be separated not in the world, but within us. How do we contribute to the evil in the world? How do we participate in healing and reconciliation? It is much easier to wait on a Messiah or to predict the Second Coming than it is to be about the courageous work of making the world a more gracious place.

Ironically, what the Jews were expecting of the Messiah is precisely what Christianity insists Jesus must do at his Second Coming. Jesus will lead an army, become the high priest, and judge the nations. The Jesus who taught his disciples to turn the other cheek and love their enemies is going to return on a white horse and declare war. The Jesus who said he had sheep in other pens was going to destroy every lamb not branded a Christian. The Jesus who died for the world was going to kill most of its inhabitants. But if he didn't do it then, why would he now? Each of these expectations relies on a dualistic view, in which destruction and separation rather than healing and unity characterize the kingdom of God.

I no longer believe in this dualism, and I no longer await a Second Coming. If Jesus returns, it will be to once more remind us of what's important—that we love our neighbors as ourselves. If Jesus comes again, it will be to convince us of the possibilities within us. Jesus said, "The one who believes in me will also do the works that I do and, in fact, will do greater works than these" (John 14:12). It's time to stop waiting and start working. It's time to complete the work Jesus began and to do even greater things.

In order for this to happen, we must abandon theologies and philosophies that destroy and separate. We must embrace ideas that heal and unite. More than ideas, we need to embrace people—those who are like us and, more important, those who are not. What we must destroy are institutions that allow us to justify and rationalize inequality, injustice, and intolerance.

In the book of Revelation, the angels of God destroy a seven-headed beast with ten crowns on his horns. Hal Lindsey identified this beast as the European Common Market, which had ten nations at the time. For Lindsey and many other dualists, human unity is always suspicious. In Lindsey's worldview, division is not only a human reality; it is the divine plan. Jesus is coming back to divide the sheep from the goats. Any human attempt to reconcile nations and overcome differences is irrelevant, if not irreverent.

I don't fear a seven-headed beast, but I have a strong loathing for the two-headed beast of sectarianism and nationalism. The merger of religious devotion and national pride has killed millions of people and continues to justify systems and actions that perpetuate an ungracious world. When I'm convinced my faith is pure and yours is evil, or that my country is right and yours is wrong, I can do beastly things. But when I recognize our common humanity and believe in our ultimate reconciliation, I am freed from the restraints of religious and national division.

In previous chapters, I've made my appeal for gracious religion, one that is gentle, humble, open, and compassionate. I've challenged Christianity to abandon its arrogance and appreciate the genuine spirituality of others. Unfortunately, religious intolerance is not solely to blame for the ugliness in the world. There is one other belief that does even more damage and that people cling to even more stubbornly than religious faith. The greatest obstacle to a gracious world is nationalism.

The Problem with
Nationalism

Our world is changing us. There was a time when people lived within their tribe, nation, or religion largely unaffected by other tribes, nations, or religions. The advent of air travel, satellite communication, and the Internet has ended such isolation forever. Information that once took months, if not years, to move from person to person and culture to culture intrudes in seconds. The Information Revolution has made us keenly aware of one another.

Awareness is only the tip of the iceberg. We are discovering, whether we like it or not, that we are interconnected. In a global economy, the decisions of one nation affect many others. Industrialization in Asia results in acid rain in Canada. A conflict in the Middle East jeopardizes the oil supply to factories in Indiana. Global awareness and interdependence are realities. A disaster in Malaysia is broadcast within minutes. A famine in Africa is documented and detailed, with daily reports on the death toll. An ethnic cleansing in the Balkans or Rwanda unfolds before our eyes. We no longer have the luxury of ignoring one another, though we continue to try.

During the negotiations over the North American Free Trade Agreement (NAFTA), many people in the United States predicted we'd be exporting jobs to Mexico. In the midst of these fears, I remember an interview with a local auto worker. He was asked what he thought of General Motors opening a plant in Mexico. He replied, "Those people don't deserve our jobs."

Though I realize his response was bred of fear, I've thought often about the self-absorption of his comment. It revealed much about our ethnocentricity. It suggested that the people of Mexico were not "our" people. We have no responsibility for seeing them employed and provided with a livelihood. It also suggested they were subhuman or immoral. They didn't deserve a good job. They deserved to live in poverty and destitution. Finally, it implied that the accidents of birth—that we happened to be born in the United States—bestowed special rights and privileges.

I remember a trip to El Paso, Texas, as a teenager. We crossed the Rio Grande and discovered ourselves in another world. A stone's throw from the glass and steel buildings of downtown El Paso were buildings made of clay, women cooking tortillas over an open fire, and children running about barefoot in raw sewage. My father made certain I saw more than the tourist traps along the main streets of Juarez. When we crossed the bridge that evening, I asked my father, "Why do people living only a few miles apart, divided by an imaginary line, live such different lives?"

My father tried to explain nationalism to me. He failed. Not because he couldn't describe this blight on humanity, but because it made no sense to me. As an adult, I still can't make any sense of it. Why should the randomness of my place of birth determine so much about the quality of my life? As a Christian, I should find this blasphemous. The worth of individuals remains constant, no matter where they were born, no matter what their race, no matter what flag flies above them.

One of the ramifications of being concerned for all people has been my opposition to self-absorbed nationalism. I understand loving the place and people with whom we live. I appreciate many of the values of our political system. I've enjoyed the blessings of living in the United States as much as anyone. Being patriotic isn't the problem. What deeply disturbs me is when patriotism becomes a rationalization for defending inequality, as if the imaginary lines we draw confer worth and dignity, as if these boundaries allow us not only to ignore the misery of others, but should they threaten our comfort, the right to destroy them.

Nationalism is patriotism without a conscience.

Chris Hedges, a veteran war correspondent, writes:

"Lurking beneath the surface of every society, including ours, is the passionate yearning for a nationalist cause that exalts us, the kind that war alone is able to deliver. It reduces and at times erases the anxiety of individual consciousness. We abandon individual responsibility for a shared, unquestioned communal enterprise, however morally dubious."[3]

He details how often the destruction of other human beings—the enemy—allows us to ignore our own shortcomings and escape our responsibilities. Sadly, when we assert "My country—right or wrong," we expose the immorality of nationalism. When our nation is given such absolute allegiance, our nation becomes our religion and our religion becomes idolatrous. A patriot must object to this perversion of our natural affection for the place and people of our birth.

To understand how destructive nationalism can be, we need only consider how many wars have been fought between "Christian" nations. In so doing, we expose our true motives—we will use anything, even God, to justify the continued prosperity and comfort of those within our borders. We are willing to kill other Christians in order to defend our interests. In the end, our national identity is more compelling than our religious commitments. No wonder, when nations of other faiths threaten or attack, we so easily wrap our flags around the cross.

Shortly after the events of September 11, several members of my Quaker meeting asked us to place the national flag in the front of our meeting room. I opposed this, reminding them of the historic Quaker tradition of peace, motivated by our conviction of the worth of all people. They grumbled a bit, but ultimately withdrew their request. Yet I believe a national flag has no business in any religious setting.

When we pledge our uncritical allegiance to a national flag, we compromise our faith.

This should be apparent by even a cursory examination of history. Germany was one of the most theologically educated, religiously observant countries in Europe in the 1930s. Hitler rose to power with the support of many in the Church. They wanted to be patriotic. Ironically, it was the fringe groups, such as the Seventh Day Adventists and the Jehovah's Witnesses, who opposed the Nazis and paid with their lives. Most churches in Germany hung a swastika near the cross. Many of the men and women who were guards in the extermination camps worshiped every Sunday. How was this possible?

The Nazis, with the support of the Church, defined everyone who wasn't Aryan as subhuman. Unfortunately, traditional dualistic theology, in which only a few are elected and favored, was easily twisted into religious justification for this evil. Only religion committed to universal concern can resist such manipulations. The reason we should resist flags in our churches is because religion must always serve as the conscience rather than the cheerleader for the nation. Whenever the nation devalues those outside or within its borders, the religious should be the first to protest.

Martin Niemoller, a German pastor who eventually resisted Hitler, wrote: "First they came for the Communists and I didn't speak up, because I wasn't a Communist. Then they came for the Jews, and I didn't speak up, because I wasn't a Jew. Then they came for the Catholics, and I didn't speak up, because I was a Protestant. Then they came for me, and by that time there was no one left to speak up for me."[4] Committing ourselves to being concerned for all people removes all our excuses for inaction. Since they are human, we are one with them.

When we are concerned for all people, no ethnic group or nation can ever claim special favor. We are citizens of the world. We must abandon any allegiance higher than our responsibility to humanity. We must adopt the Golden Rule—"Do unto others as you would have them do unto you"—as a global commitment. We must recognize how easily national pride becomes the ammunition of hate, war, and genocide. Even our language must change—the term "third world" implies a hierarchy of concern and value. We must acknowledge our participation in systems that demean and devalue the cultures of others.

This won't be easy. My friend Ivan is from Argentina. One day, after we'd been friends for nearly a year, he said, "I don't want to upset you, but there is a term you use often that offends me." Startled, I mentally reviewed our interaction, trying to discover what I could have said to offend him. I'd been careful not to use terms I knew to be derogatory.

Seeing my confusion, Ivan explained, "You are always calling your nation 'America' and calling yourself an 'American.' You don't seem to realize there are millions of Americans living in Central and South America. You have two choices. Either you can begin calling yourself a 'North

American,' or you can truly claim the people of Central and South America as your brothers and sisters."

I've decided to claim them as brothers and sisters. My patriotism must become an affection for this planet and everyone on it. All must become my compatriots. I realize this requires more than merely claiming them. It means being willing to overcome the cultural, religious, and national prejudices that have separated us. It means learning to embrace them fully as children of God.

When Jacob and Esau
Embrace

On January 25, 2002, fifty-two soldiers and officers in the Israeli army reserves published a letter declaring their refusal
to serve in the West Bank and Gaza Strip. The letter said,
"We shall not continue to fight beyond the 1967 borders [of
Israel] in order to dominate, expel, starve, and humiliate an
entire people." They argued that their commitment to the
noblest of national and religious principles made their participation impossible.

The political and public response was swift and severe.
Newspapers called them traitors. Some were demoted. Others were arrested and imprisoned. Many were ostracized by
friends and family. In a nation where suicide bombings had
become a common tragedy, there wasn't much sympathy for
the Palestinians and anyone who "sided" with them.

Yet these men, and the 480 others who soon signed their
letter of protest, were not pacifists. They were soldiers who
fully supported their country's right to defend its borders
and assure the life and liberty of its citizens. What they
could not support was the dehumanization characteristic
of the occupation of the West Bank and Gaza Strip. They

confessed to participating in and observing many acts of brutality, to practices designed to enrage and humiliate Palestinian men, women, and children. They believed the only path to peace was one in which Israelis and Palestinians began to treat each other with dignity.

In *Breaking Ranks,* Ronit Chacham interviews several of the authors of the original letter. One man, Staff Sergeant Shamai Leibowitz, explained one of the primary obstacles to peace—Jews and Palestinians didn't take their own history and theology seriously. Leibowitz explained:

> One Talmadic sage taught his students that because Jacob hurt Esau, and then Esau threatened to kill him, Esau would always hate Jacob. . . . Just as we are taught that Esau will always hate Jacob, the Palestinians will always hate Jews. If this isn't incitement, I don't know what is. Instead of teaching children the actual text, they teach them nationalist propaganda.
>
> When you read the actual text, what you find is that, despite the conflict that raged between Jacob and Esau, at the end of the day they made peace. They divided the land between them, even though Esau was the culprit, the one who threatened Jacob with murder, the "terrorist" if you will. The Bible teaches us that Esau was also a human being with compassion and sympathy, who, when respected and granted his rights, preferred peace. The Bible is

not one-sided, and humanity overcomes vengeance. It's a terrific story!⁵

The story Sergeant Leibowitz refers to, in Genesis 33, does not suggest that the enmity between the descendents of Jacob and of Esau is inevitable. When Jacob and Esau finally met, after years of estrangement and hostility, the Hebrew Scriptures say, "Esau ran to meet him, and embraced him, and fell on his neck and kissed him, and they wept" (Genesis 33:4). The story also makes it clear this reconciliation came at a price.

Jacob did not approach Esau, who he thought hated him, without preparing the way. He sent presents of goats, lambs, camels, colts, bulls, and donkeys and instructed his servants to present them to Esau. He approached Esau humbly, bowing seven times. He did this when he was yet uncertain of his brother's intent. He did this even though he could have claimed the right to defend himself and all that belonged to him. Jacob had to be willing to abandon his pride in order to be reconciled to his brother.

The solution to the impasse between Israelis and Palestinians is both simple and tremendously difficult—they both must swallow their pride. Living peacefully together must become more important than being the most righteous. Israelis must recognize the legitimate rights of Palestinians to have a nation. Why? Because they insist Palestinians must recognize the right of Israel to exist. One must take the first step and bow to the other. Then, and only then, will they be able to embrace. Without this willingness, the cycle of violence will continue and everyone will become less and less human. The two-headed beast of sectarianism and nationalism will feast on their children for generations.

What I am asking of Israelis and Palestinians is equally relevant for you and me. When we think of our enemies, personal and global, will we remember what Esau and Jacob had forgotten? We have the same father. After Jacob and Esau were reconciled, Jacob said, "Truly to see your face is like seeing the face of God" (Genesis 33:10). It is when we see God in each and every person that we finally understand our kinship. We finally find the courage to belong to the human race.

The Courage to Belong

When I was a child, I joined the church. I went to the altar one Sunday, confessed my sins, and accepted Jesus as my Lord and Savior. At the time I thought myself courageous. The preacher assured me I'd taken the most important step of my life.

It was a significant step. In becoming a Christian, I chose a way of life that honored God, valued life, and was committed to love and service. This was a much better path than self-absorption and self-gratification. I discovered the joy of being part of a community and experienced the power of working together for a common good. I don't regret either my decision or those experiences.

I do regret how long it took me to take the next step—to recognize that what I had experienced within the Church was what God desired for the world. It was so much easier to belong to a religious group, or a nation, or a class of people like me. It was so much more comfortable to surround myself with people who thought, acted, and looked like me. That didn't take much courage.

It took more courage to voice my belief that God will save every person. I knew some would think me a traitor.

There was some cost in preaching and writing of God's grace for all people. But, honestly, there has been far more joy than suffering. I don't consider this book and its ideas especially courageous.

When I think of courage, I think of Rachel Corrie. Rachel died on March 25, 2003. She was crushed by a bulldozer as she stood in front of a Palestinian house being destroyed by the Israeli military. Rachel, though dressed in an orange vest, was "accidentally" knocked down, covered with dirt, and run over repeatedly. This was after she and other protesters had stopped the demolition for three hours. Rachel was twenty-three years old.

When Rachel died, the Israeli authorities announced, "This is a regrettable incident where a group of protesters were acting irresponsibly." I disagree. I believe Rachel was being more responsible than most of us. She had accepted her responsibility to care about her Palestinian brothers and sisters. She had the courage to belong to the human race.

I think she'd also discovered the most remarkable insight of Christianity—we can live boldly because we have nothing to fear. Jesus said, "Those who want to save their life will lose it, and those who lose their life for my sake will save it" (Luke 9:24). This vision of God's love and human immortality should be a source of personal grace and courage. We can be faithful whether others are waving palm branches or fists. We can act because we're no longer waiting. We can reach out because we see the face of God in every person. We can refuse to bow to the cultural pressures that call us away from grace and goodness. We can be children of God.

I have abandoned many of the beliefs of my childhood, but I continue to believe in the resurrection of Jesus. The witness of Christianity is not that Jesus died, but that Jesus lives. I believe life is eternal. We don't have to be afraid of death or hell. We can live the life of Jesus. We can carry our crosses. We can turn the other cheek. We can walk the extra mile. We can love our enemies. We can refuse to live our lives in fear. We don't have to kill anyone to bring about the kingdom of God, but we may have to die.

My friend Harold believes we can stop the violence anywhere in the world. He says it's simple—people who are convinced of God's grace and eternal life must stand between the combatants and offer themselves as living sacrifices. He admits that many of us would die, but he's convinced what the world needs is martyrs—people willing to give witness to their faith with their lives. We need an army of men and women like Rachel Corrie.

Harold's solution reminds me of a story from the Orient:

When an advancing army stormed into a small town, a general called his scouts before him. "Where are the citizens of this village?" he demanded.

"They have all fled in fear," the scouts replied.

"Is there no one here to pay tribute?" the general shouted.

"No one but the priest. He remains in the temple."

Quickly, the general marched to the temple, burst through the doors, and demanded to see the priest. After a search, the priest was found reading quietly in his study. The general, angry that the cleric refused to greet him as conqueror, shouted, "Don't you know that you are looking at one who can run you through without batting an eye?"

"Don't you know," the priest replied, "that you are looking at one who can be run through without batting an eye."

For a moment, the soldier stared in disbelief at the priest. Then, slowly, a smile danced on his lips. He bowed low and left the temple.[6]

This ungracious world needs men and women so convinced of God's grace and the ultimate reconciliation of every person that they act courageously and confidently. They can die without batting an eye. The Bible speaks of such people. "They confessed that they were strangers and foreigners on the earth, for people who speak in this way make it clear that they are seeking a homeland. If they had been thinking of the land that they had left behind, they would have had opportunity to return. But, as it is, they desire a better country, that is, a heavenly one. Therefore, God is not ashamed to be called their God" (Hebrews 11:13–16).

Do you desire a better country and a more gracious world? Do you accept your responsibility to create heaven on earth, to recognize the kingdom of God within you and within others, to be willing to offer your life in the fulfillment of God's dream for the world? Are you willing to leave everything else behind—your comfort, your pride, your religious and national prejudices—in order to be part of this gracious world? I'm convinced if enough of us make this commitment, we can finally cross the Jordan into that promised land. I don't know the day or the hour when the kingdoms of the earth will become the kingdom of God, but I'm not waiting anymore.

In every soul, in every nation, race, and religion, God has planted the seeds of this kingdom. Some cultivate and nurture God's seed, and some do not, yet even in those lives God is working, anticipating a garden of grace, a new Eden. In the heart of this garden will stand a tree whose diverse branches shade all of God's children. When we eat of its fruit, we will not die, but will live fully, fearlessly, and forever in unity and in love.

1. Elaine Pagels, *Beyond Belief: The Secret Gospel of Thomas* (New York: Random House, 2003), p. 241. Pagels offers a modern translation of Thomas. She makes a compelling argument for valuing noncanonical writings such as Thomas.
2. Martin Luther King Jr., *Why We Can't Wait* (New York: Penguin Books, 1963), p. 86. This book, more than any other, challenged those who confused nonviolence with passivity.
3. Chris Hedges, *War Is a Force That Gives Us Meaning* (New York: Public Affairs, 2002), p. 45. Though Hedges approaches the problems of nationalism and war from a secular viewpoint, he concludes that the only answer is love.

4. Martin Niemoller, quoted in "Architect of Evil," *Time,* August 28, 1989.
5. Ronit Chacham, *Breaking Ranks* (New York: Other Press, 2003), pp. 93–94. These interviews are both chilling and moving. They offer hope that we are moving beyond the rationalization "I was just obeying orders."
6. William R. White, *Stories for the Journey* (Minneapolis, MN: Augsburg, 1988), p. 95. A collection of stories of faith and courage from all the great religious traditions.

As always, if you wish to write us, feel free. Although we can't guarantee a response, we do promise our thoughtful consideration of your comments. We can be contacted at the following address:

HarperSanFrancisco
Attn: Philip Gulley and James Mulholland
353 Sacramento Street, Suite 500
San Francisco, CA 94111–3653